The
INTERNATIONAL HEBREW HERITAGE LIBRARY

The
INTERNATIONAL
HEBREW

INTERNATIONAL BOOK CORPORATION
MIAMI, FLORIDA

HERITAGE

LIBRARY

By the Editors of
The Israeli Publishing Institute, Jerusalem, B. M.

VOLUME III:

GREAT JEWS IN ART

EDITORIAL STAFF
for the International Hebrew Heritage Library

ORY N. MAZAR
General Editor

EMIL FEUERSTEIN, Ph. D.
Contributing Editor

**GAALYAHU CORNFELD
MARVIN GROSSWIRTH**
Editorial Directors

JOSEPH JARKON
Publication Director

CAROL S. SANDERS
Managing Editor

**MILKA CIZIK
AMOS KAZIMIRSKI**
Art and Production

Table of Contents

FOREWORD

For many centuries, Jewish art was confined to the artifacts of everyday life or to the structures and appurtenances of religious activity. The Jews of old took literally the Biblical injunction against graven images, and the human form was rarely if ever shown. As emancipation of the Jew increased, so did his worldliness and, consequently, his cultural expansion and development. Some, like Pissarro, Modigliani, and Chagall, were innovators or leaders, offering the world exciting, sometimes shocking, new ideas of artistic expression. Others, true to the schools of art which they espoused, nevertheless were innovators because of their introduction to those schools of Jewish subjects. Thus, for example, though the work of Arthur Szyk is often compared to the intricacies and delicacies of the art of the ancient East, his depictions of Jewish personalities and events are uniquely his own.

It has been said that a work of art is a medium of communication between the artist and the viewer. This concept seems to be borne out by artists who have endeavored, through their art, to present to the world the agonies, the joys, the frustrations and the hopes of being a Jew.

Israel Renov, D.H.L., Ph.D.
Professor, City University of New York

ACKNOWLEDGEMENTS

The Editors wish to express their thanks to the various agencies and organizations whose invaluable assistance made this work possible. These include: The Zionist Archives, Jerusalem and New York; The Jewish National Fund, Jerusalem and New York; Keren Hayesod, Jerusalem; Beth Jabotinsky, Tel Aviv; YIVO Institute, New York; Union of American Hebrew Congregations, New York; New York Public Library; Hadassah, New York; The Nobel Foundation, Stockholm; The Leo Baeck Institute, New York; The National Foundation, New York; The New York Philharmonic Society; the Esperanto League for North America, New York; American Jewish Archives, Cincinnati; Jewish Theological Seminary, New York; and others. A detailed list of picture credits appears at the end of the Index.

Also gratefully acknowledged are the efforts and labors of Jeanne Kuebler, Eli Flatto, Barbara Northrop, and Joanna Smart for their editorial assistance; Amos Kasimirsky for work on production and layout; Charles Cassidy for special artwork; and Tove and Ira Solomon for additional research and photographs.

VOLUME III:
GREAT JEWS IN ART

MARK ANTOKOLSKY
1843-1902

Until Jewish emancipation took place during the last century and the Jewish people emerged from behind the ghetto walls the artistic talents of Jews remained undeveloped. The written word had been more important to the practice of Judaism and had taken precedence over painting and sculpture. In the synagogue itself the human form was not depicted since ancient times because it might lead to idol worship. But about 150 years ago, a few Jews entered European society as artists, either to express their Jewish heritage or their new society, or, in some cases, to portray both, pointing out their dual heritage.

Mark (Mordechai) Antokolsky, born in 1843, was the first Jewish sculptor of the modern age. Through his stone, wood and metal carvings he made the world realize that Jews were more than just the "People of the Book," and freed of restrictions, could succeed in the arts.

Antokolsky, born in the Lithuanian province of Russia, received a traditional Jewish education, but surprised his family by his artistic talent at an early age. His ability to mold materials into interesting forms was so unquestionable that he began to develop himself by serving first under a maker of gold lace, then an engraver and finally under a craftsman who taught him the techniques of wood carving. He entered the academy in St. Petersburg (Leningrad) but was so poor that he had to work much of the time to earn a living. His wood relief *The Jewish Tailor* won him a prize, and *The Miser,* an ivory relief, received much acclaim. In both pieces the intense personality of each subject is brought out by the artist's skill. He was so proud of his heritage that this early period was devoted chiefly to Jewish subjects.

Antokolsky turned to Russian themes and his name became world renowned. His masterpiece was a monumental marble statue of Ivan the Terrible, one of Russia's most powerful Czars. Ivan is shown seated on his throne dressed in his royal robes, while his face reveals the heavy burdens of power. Beside the Czar is a sceptre, the symbol of his authority. This statue was acquired by the reigning

"Spinoza" by Antokolsky

Czar Alexander, who made Mark Antokolsky a member of the Academy, an honor reserved for the finest artists.

Antokolsky's health required a warmer climate than Russia and he worked in Italy for the next eight years. During this period he created *Peter the Great,* a gigantic statue of another great Russian czar. He later carved the *Dying Socrates,* a statue of the Greek teacher in his last moments, slumped in his chair, his limbs limp and his bald head sunken on to his chest.

Antokolsky was made a Knight of the Legion of Honor. Despite this the Russian art critic Stassow wrote of him, "We are less concerned with Europe's opinion about Antokolsky than with the question of what he means to us Russians. He is the greatest sculptor of our time, and his personality differs from that of everybody else. Ever since he created *Ivan,* his fame has grown. Let us not forget that he is a Jew, and what this means in Russia. To reach his goal, he has endured sufferings such as no other race has had to bear."

Despite such tribute, there were anti-Semitic elements in Russia who resented the fact that a Jew was portraying their national heroes, and who attempted to diminish Antokolsky's prestige by writing defamatory articles about him. Angered by this and by the government-inspired massacre of Jews, Antokolsky joined the mass exodus of his people for new homes in America, Palestine and Western Europe. As an artist he was drawn to Paris, the world art center, where he spent 20 years. But even here there was no peace for him as a Jew, due to the violent anti-Semitism that occurred during the Dreyfus case. He was influenced by these times and returned to the Jewish themes which he had used in his youth. Among these is a statute of Baruch Spinoza, the Dutch-Jewish philosopher, sculpted in a meditative pose.

Antokolsky, once a humble worker in wood and ivory, ended his career as a creator of gigantic statues. Yet whether he created a Jewish tailor threading his needle, or the czar on his throne bearing the nation's destiny, Mark Antokolsky was a distinguished master of his art.

BEZALEL BEN URI
13TH CENTURY B.C.

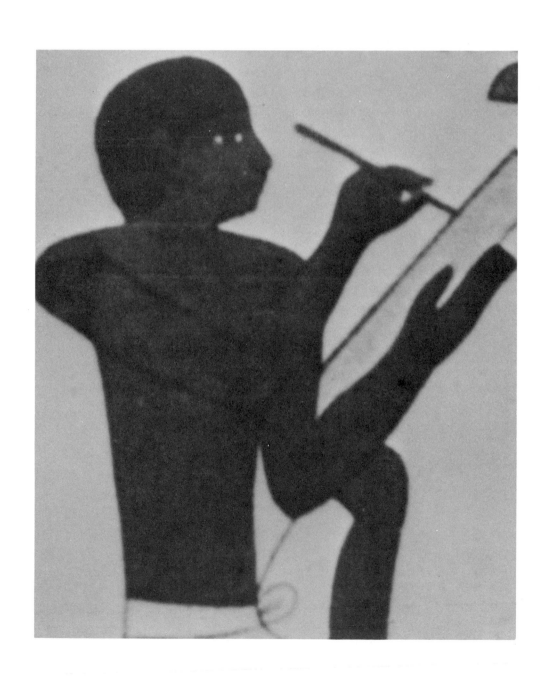

Bezalel ben Uri of the tribe of Judah is considered the first genuine Hebrew artist. Great grandson of Miriam, he was chosen by her brother Moses to create an altar for God in the desert wilderness. Not only was he to set up the Tabernacle, but he was to prepare all the implements for the sacred ritual.

The Bible relates that Bezalel was inspired "in wisdom, understanding and knowledge and in all manner of workmanship; and to devise skillful works, to work in gold, and in silver, and in brass; and in cutting of stones for setting, and in carving of wood to work in all manner of skillful workmanship."

He was assisted in the task by Ohaliab ben Achisamach of the tribe of Dan, who excelled in the same crafts. By naming Ohaliab, a member of one of the smaller and less significant tribes, to work with Bezalel, of the most populous tribe, Judah, Moses carefully averted complaints of favoritism because of his relationship with Bezalel.

Bezalel, we are told, constructed the bronze altar during the 13th century B.C.; the work seems to have survived through the centuries of struggle and settlement. We hear of it in the days of David (late 10th c. B.C.) when it appears in the Tent of Meeting, the desert shrine that preceded the building of the Temple. Even Solomon is said to have offered sacrifices to the Lord there.

Scholars believe that the Hebrews in Bezalel's time were not only familiar with the crafts of their neighbors, but followed in their steps when they built and decorated their shrines or produced other artifacts. In Egypt, where techniques and styles had not changed for centuries until the Hebrews appeared upon the scene, we find in their ancient painting many descriptions of ironsmiths along with gold and silver jewellers. The paintings even show iron plate work and the manufacture of bronze. On the tomb of Mereruko, metal workers are shown weighing bronze, smelting metals, beating gold sheet and preparing gold ornaments.

The Bible tells us that jewellers and artificers were known to be men of great wisdom, intelligence and skill in manipulating bronze and, later, iron and other metals.

A sculpture class at the Bezalel Art School in Jerusalem, named for the famous artist of antiquity

Hebrew and Phoenician craftsmen cooperated in decorating the palaces of kings and homes of the rich with ivory panels, sculptured and carved stone and delicate woodwork. From archeological discoveries, we know that Phoenician art since earliest times drew its inspiration, decorative patterns and techniques from Egypt, Crete and Cyprus. The early Israelites were exposed to the same influences and to the art of their close neighbors, the Phoenicians, which helped them create a native Israelite style.

The respect reserved for artisans is reflected in the verses of Ecclesiasticus (Ben Sira) in which the artificer is classed as one of the four craftsmen indispensable to society, the other three being the farmer, the jeweller and the potter. Small wonder then that the name of Bezalel, which in itself means "in God's shadow" was revered and respected in his own generation and in every generation thereafter. The Bezalel Art School in Jerusalem was named after this earliest of Hebrew artists, and stands as a lasting tribute to his contributions to art and to Judaism.

Artisans of ancient Egypt demonstrating some of the techniques of jewelry manufacture employed by Bezalel

JOSEPH BUDKO
1888-1940

An old Jew and his wife stand in front of their impoverished home. Every line of their stance, every wrinkle in their clothing is traced in a profound sadness and weary resignation. Here are two humble, ashen-faced Jews, standing beside a dilapidated fence which cuts them off from a green, flowery meadow. All exiled Jewry, separated from its heritage, is symbolized in these two figures.

Budko's special value lies in his attempt to capture the essence of his view of life which lies in the world of Judaism, in the landscape of his town, and in the world of Jewish culture and religion. Budko paints teachers, rabbis, scholars and students, especially students. He depicts them with long pointed hands and fingers, their faces half-hidden by the darkness of the *beis hamedrash*. The light in Budko's etchings is usually that of candles — at home on Sabbath or in the synagogue. Only their scanty light illuminates the rabbi's face and the faces of scholars instructing their attentive students. Only the dim light of a candle kindles the face of a poor student or illumines the woman making the blessing over Sabbath candles, her husband making *havdala*.

Joseph Budko was born in Plonsk, Poland, where he went to *heder* (a small school). After his bar-mitzva the road led to Vilna where he continued his religious studies, attended the Reali secular school and also found time for lessons at an art school. This three-pronged approach of Judaism, secular knowledge and art was to be followed until his death.

After finishing at Reali, he continued his studies only in art school. He went from Vilna to Berlin (in 1910) where he expended prodigious effort to learn the technical aspects of graphic art, attending classes at the city's Museum for Art Work and special lessons for metal engraving and other metal work. While in Berlin, he amassed a deep knowledge of carving, and during his four years in Vilna and four in Berlin he was busy developing his talent in bronze etching. In 1914 his artistic development began in earnest as he drew heads and figures and prepared graphic reproductions of drawings that impressed him. In 1916, he received his first art

"The Scholar" by Joseph Budko

assignment: to completely illustrate the Passover Haggadah.

Budko began as all other Jewish graphic artists had — from the Haggadah — he introduced a completely new form of the Hebrew letter, utilizing the decorative value of the Hebrew alphabet while weaving it into pictures. *Had Gadya* (One Kid), for instance, depicts a wanderer walking in the desert, dragging behind him a little goat that knows it is being prepared for slaughter. A miniature picture, with two letters, a man and a kid — constitutes a complete tragedy. Perhaps the wanderer is fate while the small, weak kid is, perhaps, man. The story is crystallized in this tiny picture.

After the Haggada, other work came his way in abundance, including series of illustrations for books written by Jewish authors: Frishman, Peretz, Shalom Aleichem and Shalom Asch.

A street scene by Budko

Budko's self-portrait

Budko later applied his talents to Ex Libris, a field of art unknown hitherto among the Jews. His first Ex Libris — a landscape of Israel in 1911 and a view of a road in 1912 — was the beginning of a rich and varied series. Usually, Ex Libris artists begin with woodcuts, then work up to bronze cuts or other types of etchings. Budko, however, began from bronze and came to woodcuts only after much work with the stronger material. His woodcuts are unforgettable: *Dream, Jeremiah Consoling Rachel,* and above all, illustrations for the *Book of Psalms.* Here he reached a high point of artistic fulfillment, with such illustrations as *On the Banks of Babylon, Open for Me the Gates of Righteousness,* and *Come, Let us Sing.* Here, as in the Haggadah, initials intertwined with pictures, and ancient Jewish musical instruments, folklore, symbolism and simple meanings for the works, are all incorporated.

One of Budko's specialties is his portrayals of East European Jewry. Here we see eternal faces, pictures that relate the whole story of Jewish life outside Israel, full of sorrow and joy. The subjects' eyes are windows through which we peek, and view that world in all its depth. The sentiment or pathos usually seen in similar subjects drawn by other artists is lacking here, instead we see a serious, profound picture of the true Jewish atmosphere, a picture of life as it was in those times.

MARC CHAGALL
1887-

Every artist abides by his own guiding principles. Marc Chagall enunciated his when he was thirty-five years old and wrote: "I was born in Vitebsk, and again in Paris. My parents were farmers. I do not hate anything so much as intellectualism."

"Modern art is sick and poor," Chagall said. "The younger generation has not produced artists of great stature to take the places of the old ones... They dissect everything as they explain, comment and elucidate. This destroys spontaneity." According to Chagall, the true artist does not interest himself in "isms" nor does he try to determine the stream to which he belongs. He works diligently and leaves it to the next generation to decide to which school his work belongs. "It is forbidden for an artist to hide things. Without artifice, with complete honesty, he must relate everything as he sees and feels it."

Like the great Hebrew poet Bialik who always "drew from the same flask" of his childhood, Chagall always draws from his own childhood in the small White Russian town of Vitebsk where he first saw the world. The sights he saw then — the poor wooden houses, the large church in the center, the outskirts where the Jews lived, father, mother, aunts, uncles, a few tradesmen, many poor people, musicians with their fiddles, studious men true to God and their Torah, chickens, a horse and cart — these varied sights accompany him in all his works. Painters by nature do not speak with ease; their power is in their brush. When Chagall is asked to explain some "problem" in his work he answers, "I am describing Father and Mother." The answer may not satisfy the person asking, but it reveals the artist's "secret." The child Chagall opening his eyes and seeing the world for the first time was filled with enough excitement and wonder to last all his life.

Chagall does not view the outer aspects of the world. Instead, he sees the heart of matters. He sees Jews living in towns in which they are really apart. In a painting he depicts, for example, a Jew with a Torah scroll in his hand against a background of snow. Behind are hints of wooden houses in a foreign landscape. At his side, a

One of Chagall's many studies of circus performers

Chagall's earlier works were more realistic in form

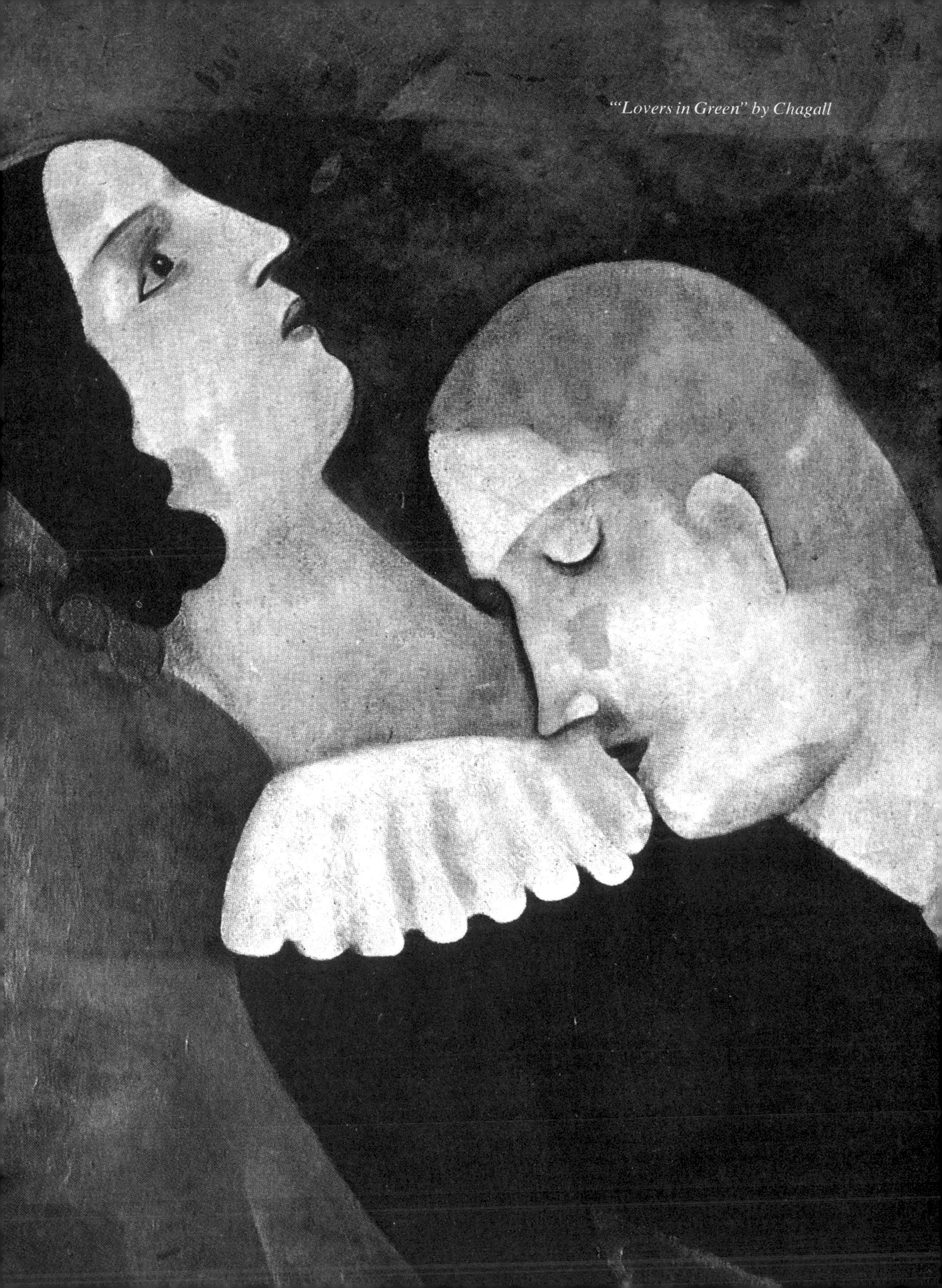

"'Lovers in Green" by Chagall

One of Chagall's many versions of Jewish fiddlers

Jewish goat. The Jew seems to be growing as he walks; detached, strangely cut off from the surrounding scenery. There is no symbolism here but stark realism as conveyed by a great artist, who has combined visual poetry and allusion, symbol and beauty. No

Chagall's "Jew Carrying the Torah"

wonder that the Jew in the painting is walking on rooftops, for the "golut" (Diaspora) village is nothing but a temporary dwelling on a long journey home. This seems like surrealism, but it is the realism of Jews in exile.

Despite their oddness, Chagall's first painting were well received; the revolutionary spirit in art had prepared critics and the public for anything. In addition, the young artist from Russia surprised Parisian critics with his great technical ability. Not every picture in this first group was difficult to understand. A few were even "normal" except for a few surprising elements, such as the fetus in the horse's womb in the monumental work of the horse dealer on his cart or the miniature picture of a soldier dancing with a girl as seen in the eyes of that very same drunken soldier, or Russian landscapes with figures wafting through the air. With the murals he drew on the walls of the Jewish Camari Theater in Moscow in 1919-20, Chagall reached a peak of power and wildness almost unmatched in art. Men, some with *tfillin,* danced on their hands; heads, hands and feet grew in the air; animals, birds and caricatures mixed and turned on the walls.

Why did Chagall draw in this way? Do pictures such as these have content and meaning? What is their uniting force? All pictures portray some aspect of reality, though often in ways to which we are not accustomed. Freud taught us that repressed, frustrated desires lurk in our minds, that these erupt at various times, especially in dreams and fantasy.

Chagall, then, is a painter of dreams. Usually we ignore dreams, as society has taught us to do. Artists, like children, however do not follow society's rules, and in their refusal to accept them, enrich our lives by bringing us to our roots.

At the end of this generation, people will be able to look back and see the deepest, most hidden desires of this man as well as the depth of his creativity. This is Marc Chagall's contribution to his generation and to the Jewish nation, a clear picture of the Jewish national character as seen in all its depth and infinite variety.

JO DAVIDSON
1883-1951

Afoot and lighthearted I take to the open road,
Healthy, free, the world before me,
The long brown path before me leading to wherever I choose.

These lines from a poem by Walt Whitman were often quoted by the sculptor Jo Davidson, and are expressive of his life.

Jo Davidson might be called a "plastic historian," who set down the history of his generation in the form of sculptures. Among those who sat for him were some of the most important statesmen, authors, scientists, and personalities of our time, such as Ghandi, Anatole France, Einstein, Roosevelt, Rockefeller and Helen Keller.

Davidson seemed to breathe life into his materials, and strove for more than mere resemblance between the model and his statue. He always tried to reveal the essential character of the model. Therefore, his model did not have to sit motionless while he worked, but could move around, speak, or do anything he wanted. On one occasion, the great scientist, Albert Einstein, asked Davidson how he managed to capture the inner personality of his subject.

"It's as if you've peeked under my skin," Einstein observed.

"I don't peek," answered Davidson, "I smell things, like a dog."

"I do that, too," Einstein said, "and you'll be surprised to learn that often I make mistakes."

Jo Davidson was deeply impressed by Helen Keller and he said of her, "She does more with the tips of her fingers than art critics do with their eyes. She passed her fingers slowly over a bust and made many profound observations."

Jo Davidson firmly believed that the artist must not isolate himself in "ivory tower" seclusion. He was always interested in what was happening in the world around him. With the outbreak of the first world war, Davidson rushed to the front lines of Belgium, where he saw all the horrors of war. He wrote of this experience and of its effect on his work: "For me, war is no longer a word in history books. I have seen it with my eyes. I now want to express in clay the great tragedy of war." The result was Davidson's creation of

Jo Davidson working on a bust of World War I hero General John J. Pershing

a relief depicting the flight of refugees on the roads, and the statue *Call to Arms,* a figure of the goddess of war raising her hands to heaven, pleading for mercy.

Jo Davidson was born on the East Side of New York. "The memories of my childhood are vague and dim," he wrote. "I remember long and gloomy halls, crowded flats, sour, strange smells, dirty, unpainted walls, and constantly moving from one place to another."

He held many jobs. He was first a newspaper boy, then an apprentice to a painter, and later an errand boy in a factory and book store. At the same time, he studied art in the evenings. Davidson's family opposed his aspirations to become an artist. For a while he yielded and began to study medicine, but the attraction of art was so strong that finally he began to work as an assistant in the Holbein Studio in New York at a salary of $ 4 a week.

Until the age of 30, Davidson lived as an impoverished artist. During this time he often questioned his own motivations for wanting to be an artist. He wrote, "I thought about it much, about my interest in sculpting busts of people. I could not say that their faces gave me an inner urge to sculpt. I did not want to sculpt merely for the sake of sculpting. Rather, it was the people themselves who interested me. To sculpt a bust there must be two people, and the important thing is the relationship between the artist and his subject."

Between the two world wars, Davidson wandered through three continents — North America, Europe and Africa, and paid two visits to the Soviet Union. At the same time, he continued to make "plastic history" for his era. During World War II, Davidson gave full expression to the heroic battle against Nazism in his statue *Lidice*. In 1944, he headed the committee of artists and scientists who worked for Roosevelt in the election campaign. In 1948, he participated in founding the Progressive Party and promoted the candidacy of Henry Wallace for the presidency.

Jo Davidson visited Warsaw, and was struck by the dimensions of the Jewish tragedy. Later, in Israel, he summarized his impressions of this visit: "After I saw what remained of the Warsaw Ghetto, the State of Israel confirmed my belief in the victory of life. The people of Israel resemble the legendary Phoenix which returns and grows limbs and lives after it has been consumed by fire — an ancient people, young in spirit among the nations, which is no longer afraid of persecution or discrimination, breathing the air of freedom and toil."

SIR JACOB EPSTEIN
1892-1964

What a curious family is Stein!
There is Gert and there's Ep and there's Ein.
Gert's poems are bunk
Ep's statues are junk
And nobody understands Ein.

This limerick printed in one of the English weeklies expresses the negative attitude which existed in England for over forty years toward the sculptures of the outstanding Jew, Jacob Epstein. What storms his work aroused! In 1908 when the Medical Association commissioned eighteen symbolic figures for their London building, such a tempest was raised that Scotland Yard had to intervene. An officer was sent to climb up the building in order to view Epstein's figures more closely. When he came down he summed up his impression in one word: Obscene!

Fifteen years later, Epstein exhibited his bronze statue *Jesus Christ*. This time the Church led the attack: "This is the face of a degenerate god, of an African, an Asiatic, an American Indian or a Hindu, a long-starving Jew, a bald Egyptian, but not Jesus."

In 1912, in the famous Père Lachaise Cemetery, a statue was placed over the grave of the wild, unhappy poet Oscar Wilde, and it too raised protests and sharp public controversies. In 1925 he was asked to prepare a statue for the grave of the famous English writer, W. H. Hudson, whose favorite subjects were nature and wild life. Epstein, in a gigantic stone relief, made a highly-stylized representation of one of Hudson's most beautiful and beloved heroines, Rima, Queen of the Birds. This once again caused scandal through his work, over which paint was poured and a swastika drawn.

Twenty years later, the attitude in England towards Epstein had not changed, for when he offered his sculpture *Lucifer* to the Tate Gallery it was politely refused. In 1950, full of bitterness because of the lack of appreciation towards his work, he was asked why he did not move somewhere else. He answered, "They will finally recognize me, but I will have to be eighty years old at least for that."

Epstein's sculptures are characterized by a blending of symbolism and realism

He was not very wrong. He was already past seventy when he first began to be recognized. The Queen of England knighted him and it began to be said that he was the greatest sculptor of the twentieth century and not the greatest Jewish sculptor as had been claimed before.

Epstein was born in New York of Russian immigrant parents. He went to Paris when he was twenty-two. But in the realm of sculpture Rodin ruled supreme and unchallenged and Epstein's efforts went unnoticed. Perhaps it was this that made him move to London. In any case he had the courage to express himself regardless of the attitude of the public. He was a daring innovator, using primitive art, ancient Egyptian and African sculpture as inspiration. Most of his work was on a monumental scale, but he was equally gifted in portraits. Famous people of the time came to him knowing that they would be perpetuated in history through the bronze image Epstein created.

Epstein was a complicated, multi-faceted personality. As a realistic portrait sculptor and a monumental symbolist, he was a revolutionary, a daring experimenter, fighting the world for decades and never yielding to the mass taste.

He was also a proud Jew. When he heard about the Jewish Legion being formed to re-conquer the ancient homeland he joined up. His widow later donated his original plaster casts to the Israel Museum in Jerusalem, and he was thus, after his death, able to return to his origins and be held in deserved honor.

YEHUDA EPSTEIN
1870-1945

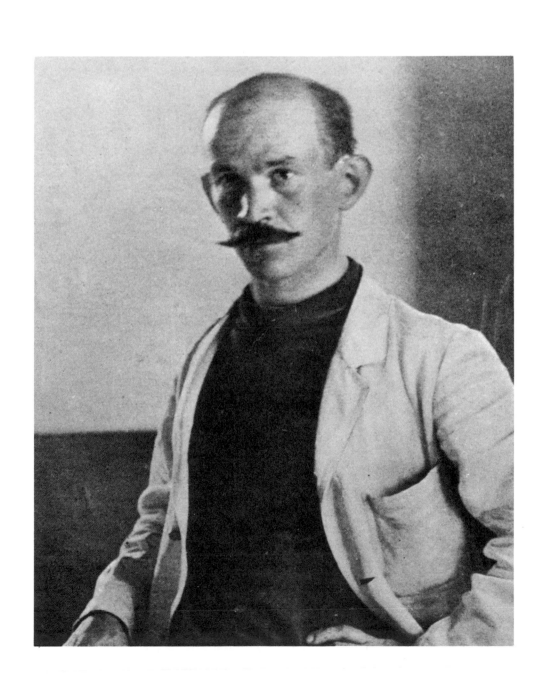

"Shh — Shh, quiet, everybody! Let me read it out loud!" Almost every Jew in that little Russian town had gathered around. It wasn't every day that a letter arrived from as far away as Berlin! Their faces filled with amazement and wonder as they listened to the closing sentence: "...and Dr. Herzl could not take his eyes off it, and finally he bought it." The group crowded around Yehuda Epstein's father clapping him on the back with congratulations. "Now what do you think of your somewhat little doodler?"

That evening the story was repeated in a hundred homes. The men told their wives the great news: "Do you remember little Yehuda, the boy who loved to draw? He not only won first prize for a painting at a Berlin competition but Theodor Herzl was there and saw the picture — a picture of Saul and David — he liked it so much he bought it! Dr. Herzl himself! Imagine!"

Yehuda Epstein became an artist quite by chance. Like most of the Jewish boys in White Russia his religious studies began when he was only five years old. The young students studied from dawn to nightfall. Time was so dear that even lunch was brought to them at the classroom. In the spare time they did have, the older boys used to play cards. The same cards were used over and over, becoming filthy and torn. Poor people couldn't dream of buying a new set so young Yehuda made a new set of cards, drawing each one by hand. In doing so he discovered a whole new world. He soon learned of schools where one could learn how to draw professionally and he knew nothing could keep him at home. He had to learn to draw! When Yehuda was 17 he went off on his own to Vilna to enroll at a drawing school much against his father's will. His talent was soon discovered and he received a scholarship. After a year at that school, he decided to learn more about art than just drawing; his heart was now set on going to one of the great academies. However, it was practically impossible for a Jew to enroll in the academy of St. Petersburg, the cultural capital of Russia, so he went to Vienna where he studied art for three years.

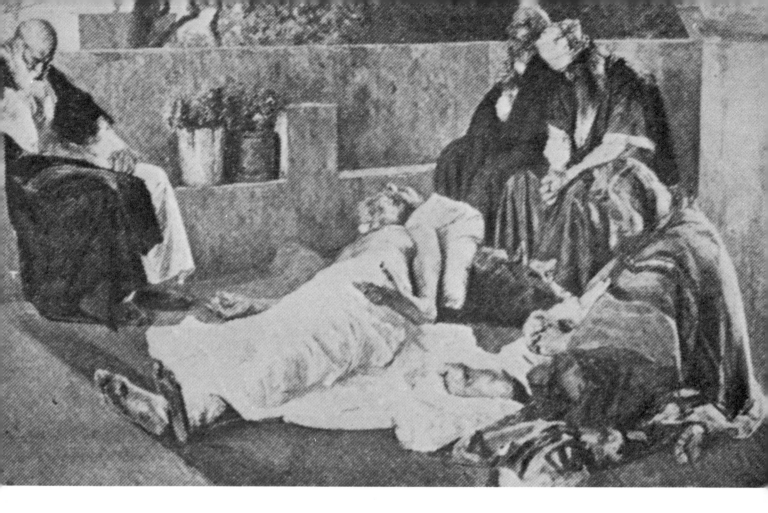

"Job" by Yehuda Epstein

His first painting revealed his interest in Jewish subject matter and won a prize. It was called *Polish Jews Playing Chess*. He continued to call on his Jewish background for inspiration, and his next work was *Saul and David,* which won him the first prize at the Berlin competition, as well as the great compliment from Theodor Herzl. Four years later, he won another prize in Berlin.

Yehuda Epstein's work is full of color, which is sometimes put on the canvas in large splotches. In his drawings, he was able to create, using simple black and white, the impression of color and the illusion of space. In this way he was like Rembrandt, and, like that great Dutch artist he chose the simplest subjects from everyday life — a corner of a room, a lantern in the market place — and turned the subject into something unique and moving by employing the effects of light. When color was added it was as though Epstein's powers were doubled and his passion unleashed. Yehuda Epstein was devoted to the Jewish people and wanted to immortalize them against the scenes he loved. But the Jewish religion forbids the making of images. "I am tired of using plaster heads as models, I would love to paint a beautiful Jewish head from life; but so far it has been almost impossible to convince a religious Jew to serve as a model," he once complained.

In addition to the prize-winning *Saul and David*, Epstein painted many other biblical subjects; he also depicted the story of the Maccabees. His paintings have become an important part of the Jewish heritage.

HENRYK GLICENSTEIN
1870-1942

In Rome, the former art capital of the world, a yeshiva boy who had known nothing outside of the world of holy books until he was 17 gained international fame. Henryk (Enrico) Glicenstein, a Jewish-Polish artist, began his studies in Munich, and at the age of 25 arrived in Rome, where he became a sensation. He won many prizes at exhibits and his works were given honored places in museums. Three of the most important men in Italy — the Pope, the King and Mussolini — eagerly posed for his busts of them. Glicenstein worked in stone, marble, bronze and wood; he also drew, painted and etched. He could change his style and medium with lightning speed and ease.

Although he was made a professor at the Warsaw Academy, he did not like his homeland's capital and hurried back to Rome, where he lived for 16 years, earning the highest award for excellence, the Order of the Crown. When Mussolini joined forces with Hitler in World War II, the artist returned the medal. In 1928 he moved to the United States.

A fellow artist pointed out that the one thing missing from Enrico's life was tranquillity. He has been severely shaken by World War I and it was no coincidence that for the years from 1915-1917, he was too disturbed to create even a single sculpture. The plight and suffering of the Jews in World War II influenced him so much that he again lost his powers of concentration.

Glicenstein's huge statues testify to his great and varied skills. Fierce strength glistens from the eyes of *Bar Kochba,* the larger-than-life hero who seems ready to attack anyone who dared threaten his nation. *Bar Kochba* stood in his studio on Rome's Via Marguta opposite the fair *Shulamit,* the gentle girl with a fragile flower in one hand and the hand of a skipping child in her other. In the back of the studio stood *Cain and Abel,* a portrayal of the first murderer in the world sending his piercing gaze heavenward while his brother lies stricken by his hand. The block on which Abel lay, face down, arms spread as if pleading for help, was inscribed in

Glicenstein at work in his studio

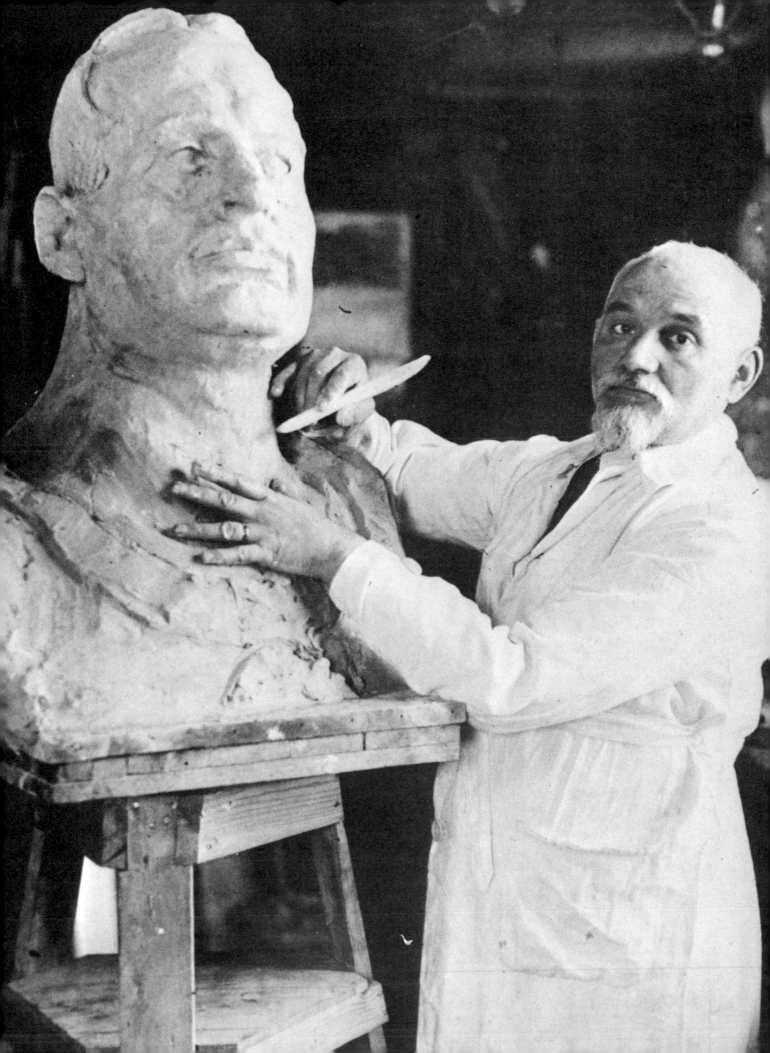

Greek: "Is this death?" as if Cain were studying this mysterious matter.

Glicenstein's son, Enrico Romano, also an artist, always carried a Bible as a source of inspiration and used to recite psalms to himself while working. His greatest dream was to create a full series of sculptures of all the heroes of the Bible. While in London in the early 1920's Glicenstein began working on the Book of Samuel. King Saul and the young David were the central figures with the prophet Samuel standing by. Glicenstein spent great effort in planning this ambitious project. When some of these Biblical works were later shown in London, the originality of interpretation and the freshness of technique won critical acclaim. When they were exhibited at the Royal Palace, critics marveled at their great balance and planning, comparing them with Phidias' work in the Parthenon.

The artist came to America in order to find supporters to aid him in the continuation of his project, but the welcome given him was far from overwhelming. Indifference, however, did not deter him and Glicenstein went on with his monumental work. One after the other, the spirit and deeds of his forefathers came to life. He dove into the depths of his nation's history in order to explain its present. He always felt the terrible sufferings of his people whether it was in Poland, where as a youth he had lived through military pogroms, or in Italy, where he had been witness to the rise of Fascism, or in America, from where he heard of his people being trampled upon by the Nazis. He used all the artistic tools at his command to express his anger. The last ten years of his life were devoted to creating statues in wood of such subjects as *The Wandering Jew, I Am a Jew, The Spanish Revolutionary* and *National Defense.*

A Pavia art professor once compared Glicenstein with a mountain whose peak can be seen and appreciated only from a certain perspective. Since his tragic death in an auto accident in 1942, we have learned to value the great and varied talents of Henryk Glicenstein, his artistic integrity and powers and his devotion to his nation.

MAURYCY GOTTLIEB
1856-1879

"Toward the end of the year I made a solemn vow to devote all my efforts to my unhappy people. I remembered the synagogue. I find it difficult to define the state of mind I was in at my studio. At times I seemed to hear the voices of members of my family long dead. Their eyes seemed to entreat me and beg, bring us back to life. Some of these long-deceased I painted from memory, while others I reproduced from photographs."

This is how the painter Maurycy (Moshe) Gottlieb described the genesis of his monumental painting, *Yom Kippur in the Old Synagogue,* which has hung in the Tel Aviv Museum since 1939. The picture shows a group of Jews at prayer. Although the group is made up of old people and children, men and women, they appear so united in worship that they seem almost a single entity. Even the wall that physically separates the women's gallery from the men's section does not disrupt their spiritual unity. The wall below the women's gallery bears the inscription: "Rise, O Lord, let Your enemies be dispersed and those that hate You flee before You."

In the center of the composition, next to the Torah scroll, the artist has painted himself, clad in the traditional tallith, the prayer shawl. The painting symbolizes Gottlieb's complete identification with his people's suffering and hopes. Although the artist painted this masterpiece when he was only 23 years old, the mantle covering the Torah scroll in the painting bears the legend: "Donated in memory of the late Moshe Gottlieb." The artist explained, "Nobody lives forever." But the inscription was, in fact, prophetic, for the young painter died that year, apparently by his own hand.

Despite the brief span of his life, Gottlieb was one of the finest Jewish painters of the 19th century and his paintings are remembered to this day. His art is characterized by rich yet delicate colors and meticulous attention to details of dress and facial expression. He saw great nobility in the faces and figures of simple Jews at

prayer. To him the *tallith,* the shawl which the Jew wraps around himself for prayer, was no less an object of beauty than the toga of the Greeks and Romans. In "Yom Kippur," his last painting, the artist created a monument to one of the loftiest ideals of Jewish spiritual life, that of Teshuva, or repentance. His genius transcended romanticism and enabled him to give expression to the spiritual essence of the Day of Atonement.

Maurycy Gottlieb was born in Galicia, and studied at the Cracow Academy of Art, where he was a student and personal friend of the Academy's director, Jan Matiko, a renowned painter in his own right. Matiko often gave the young artist additional instruction. Later Gottlieb lived in Lwow, Vienna, and Munich. His paintings aroused antagonism in the anti-Semitic press of Vienna. The critics of Viennese journals claimed that the artist contrived to "idealize" Jewish life, denying the fullness of the spiritual life portrayed by Gottlieb. They could not however deny his artistic ability.

Gottlieb's creative period in the 1870's coincides, with the beginning of the Haskalah, the era of Jewish enlightenment in Poland. Among his other notable paintings are *Uriel da Costa, Judith,* and *Shylock and Jessica,* a masterpiece of the romantic period and one of Gottlieb's best works from a technical point of view.

NAHUM GUTMANN
1898-

Nahum Gutmann, Israel's most beloved painter, once wrote: "I paint from impressions gathered by watching the panorama and by absorbing the life around us." Fascinated by the natural beauty of his native Palestine, Gutmann enlivened numerous canvasses with his fresh vision of this ancient land.

His paintings provide a visual history of the development of the Jewish nation, from the pioneering days before and during World War I to the defense of settlements against Arab harassment in the 1920's, and the building of modern Tel Aviv.

Gutmann's early impressions had perhaps the most decisive effect on his artistic style. As a child, he would go with his father to the town of Jaffa and watch with excitement and wonder the hurly-burly life of this little sea coast town. As a mature artist, he conveyed his childlike vision in *Jaffa Market,* which is alive and bristling with people hurrying to prayer, bickering over prices, or simply taking in the sun. Despite the harsh realities of life in Palestine, he always retained his belief in the ultimate goodness of mankind, and his paintings, in the words of a New York Times critic, "envelop you with a festive spirit".

Gutmann has the rare distinction of being one of the very first students at the Bezalel Art School and, in 1914, the owner of the first art studio in Tel Aviv. Moreover, he was the first illustrator of books published in Israel, his most notable achievement being the illustrations prepared for Bialik's poems and books of legends.

Gutmann's perceptiveness found expression via the pen as well as the brush. During the War of Independence, he traveled through the countryside with Israeli soldiers and the impressions he gleaned were collected in a distinguished book entitled *Ca-eleh Hayu* (They Were Like This). In his introduction to this captivating work, Gutmann wrote, "Spring was in full bloom. The fighters, burdened by fatigue and loaded with ammunition, looked this way and that and actually, they weren't anything more than children with wild hair and smiling eyes."

His natural optimism and simplicity of style are evident in an-

"Haifa Harbor" by Gutman

other work, *A Road of Orange,* in which he wrote, "If I succeed in the first chapter — I will write a second and so on until I finish."

In still another book, *The Completely Blue Donkey,* Gutmann established himself as one of the all-time great masters of children's story writing. Generations of Israeli youths have been brought up on his tales. In tribute to one of his many contributions to children's literature, Gutmann was honored with the International Andersen Prize.

Gutmann's clarity of vision, his love of life, of Israel and its remarkable people was best expressed by the artist himself who, reflecting on his painting *Jaffa Market,* said, "How fantastic life looks when you see it through a simple fisherman's net."

Nahum Gutman in his studio

SAMUEL HIRSZENBERG
1865-1908

Not many people know the name Samuel Hirszenberg, but millions are familiar with his painting *Golus* (Exile), which depicts a pathetic caravan of Jewish refugees from East Europe, patiently following their rabbi through the snow-covered wastes of the Russian plains. Among them is a small girl with large eyes, holding an old tea-kettle in her frozen hands.

There are perhaps greater artists than Hirszenberg, who are more profound in their content and approach, but none of them has reached such a level of folk-art popularity.

Hirszenberg made his painting easy to understand. He does not require great concentration or deep understanding; the viewer does not have to probe endlessly to appreciate the significance of the artistic creation before him. Every Jew who has a feeling for Jewish suffering identifies wholeheartedly with these pictures. The pathos of his painting is that of folk plays and folk stories.

Samuel, son of a poor Jewish weaver in Lodz, Poland, did surprisingly well in art lessons at school; at the age of 15 he left the city with a monthly allowance of 25 rubles, allotted by several philanthropic art lovers, and went to art school in Cracow, where he suffered all the hunger and privation usually associated with the very talented. When his scholarship expired, he began a period of bitter struggle. Matters became so bad that in Munich he was forced to sell his first large painting for almost nothing. His first success, which put an end to his hand-to-mouth existence, won him

"Fleeing the Pogrom" by Hirszenberg

"The Yeshiva" by Hirszenberg

a silver medal. This was *The Yeshiva Boys,* shown at a large international exhibition in Paris.

This success led to others and he eventually became a well-known artist, whose dramatic drawings — *Uriel Acosta* and *The Jewish Cemetery* — traveling from one exhibit to another, aroused particular public interest and received exceptionally good reviews.

Hirszenberg, as a Jew, returned to the country of his youth perhaps to achieve eminence in the town where he had once been poor and wretched. Picture after picture came off the palette, some full of pity and faith, others lamenting the fate of the Jewish people, but in all of them there is an overriding quality of the cruelty of nature accompanied by the pathos of the Jewish soul. *The Poor Jew, The Burial Place, Sabbath Afternoon* — all are pictures of different aspects of the same theme, *golus*.

Hirszenberg was a Jew with burning desires, with a glowing love for Judaism and a deep attachment for Israel. Three years after the first Zionist Congress in Basel in 1897, he immigrated to Israel and worked as an art teacher at the Bezalel Art School. For eight years he lived in Jerusalem amid the ancient colors and stones of mystic scenes, the ageless hills and mountains of the Eternal City. The artist died when he was 43 of a stomach ailment caused by his hungry childhood days. His personal suffering had paved the way for his understanding of the nation's suffering. His entire life was dedicated to the dying beauty of the ghetto. His desire was to show the world the constant struggle of the inhabitants of the ghetto to reach spiritual heights. His picture of the 17th-century sceptic Uriel Acosta captures the mental torment of those who could not always accept the ghetto morality .

Overbearing pain is recorded in *The Eternal Jew,* a sad, moving picture that created a great deal of emotion in Warsaw and Paris. *Golus* testifies to Hirszenberg's technical power of concentration and the complete control of the artist in depicting faces — not only technical prowess but psychological insight as well as an historian's view of a culture — and the picture will undoubtedly stand as an important document of the history of this period.

JOSEPH ISRAELS
1824-1911

Joseph Israels was born in Holland, the son of very religious Jewish parents. Until he was 15, young Joseph studied only the Torah and religious subjects, for his parents hoped he would become a rabbi. But the lad yearned to be an artist, although orthodox Jews believed God's commandment, "Thou shalt have no graven images," forbade the depiction of human figures. When he was 16, however, he was permitted to study at the Amsterdam Art Academy. Five years later he moved on to Paris, where he began to specialize in painting historical and Biblical subjects.

Israels might have continued to work in this vein, perhaps never realizing his full potential, if illness had not overtaken him when he was still in his twenties. He was forced to return to Holland to convalesce. There he settled for a time in a small fishing village, and became interested in painting the people around him — fishermen, farmers and artisans. He became aware of the nobility and beauty in the lives of these simple folk, and sought to convey these qualities through his painting. He also strived to commit to canvas the uniquely soft and hazy quality of the sunlight in his native land.

Soon Israels' health improved and he returned to the city streets of his youth. His new awareness and his own intense knowledge of Jewish life combined with his outstanding talent and resulted in some of the most sensitive paintings of simple Jewish life ever achieved. A typical painting shows a narrow ghetto street lined by little overhanging houses, looking as if they might lean a bit more and topple down. A storekeeper sits in the doorway of his shop. He is almost ugly, but the melancholy in his face seems to transcend the sorrows of his own life, representing instead the centuries of suffering of the Jewish nation. The style is realistic, but there is something so sensitive and so lyrical about his work that Max Liebermann once wrote that only a poet could describe Israels' paintings, since they were really poems in color.

Israels is considered the most significant figure in Dutch art since the 17th century, and the nearest in spirit to Rembrandt, on

"The Cottage Madonna" by Israels

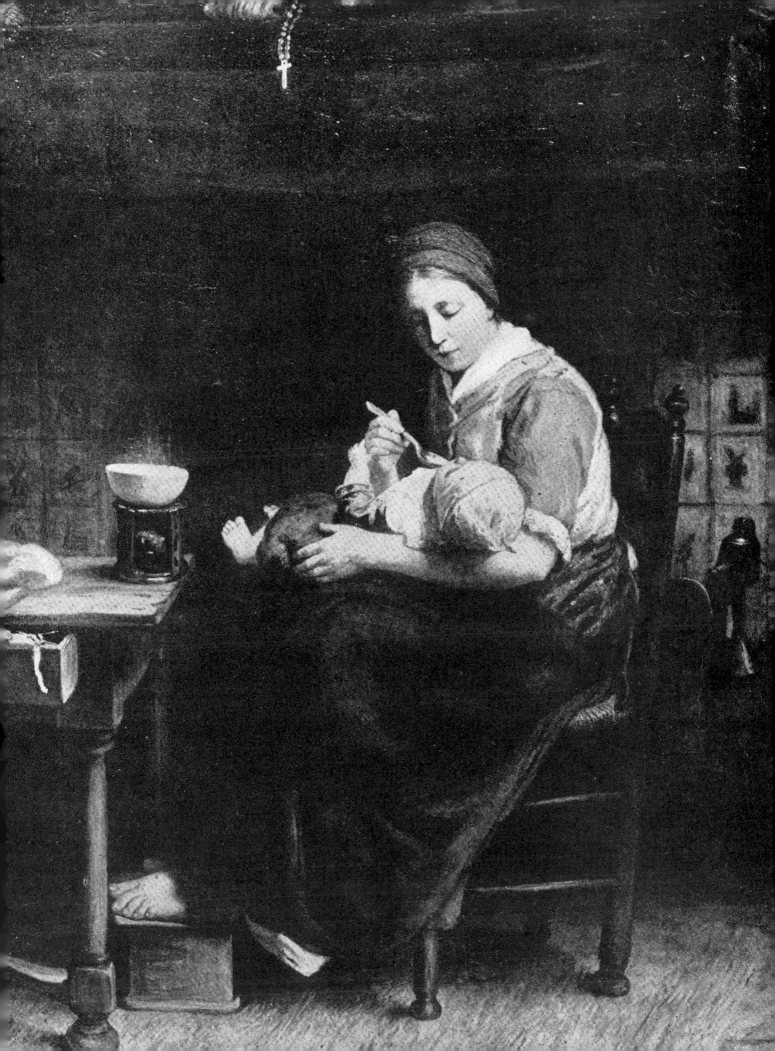

whom he modeled himself. An important difference between them is that Israels was not merely an observer of Jewish life, he was a devoted participant. The struggle to remain faithful to Judaism and also to his art remained a conflict throughout his life. He once wrote of meeting an elderly author in Spain, an orthodox Jew with whom he spoke in Hebrew, the only language they had in common. The old man knew nothing of art, only that it was prohibited. Yet Israels believed that, like the author's, his work was also holy. Years later Israels painted himself as that old writer, to show their essential sameness of spirit. As an old man, the artist told to Nahum Sokolov, the Zionist leader, his special feeling about his religion:

"You want to bring Jews to the land of Israel? Oh, a very

"Returning from the Fields" by Israels

"Carpenter," etching by Israels

hard thing to do, but lovely. On the life of my soul, a very beautiful thing. If I weren't an old man, I would go to the land of Israel myself."

Israels achieved honor and recognition during his own lifetime, unlike many artists of his generation. His 80th and 85th birthdays were celebrated as Dutch national holidays and when he died his funeral ceremony and cortege resembled that of royalty. His work is well represented in European and American museum collections.

MANE KATZ
1894-1962

"In 1924, I held an exhibition in one of Paris' larger galleries," Mane Katz once related. "Not much interest was shown and while waiting for the crowd that never came, I dozed off. Suddenly I woke up — someone was walking in the hall. From the way he inspected the pictures I knew he was an artist. After looking at my work he just walked out and immediately afterwards the director of the gallery shook my hand and said, 'Congratulations!'

" 'What happened?' " I asked him in surprise.

" 'That was Picasso. He showed a great interest in your work. You are, after all, unknown.' "

If it is at all possible to define Mane Katz, perhaps the term "Modern Hasid" fits best — a modern Hasid both in his sources of inspiration and in his relationship to the world and to man. In Katz, these Hasidic traits are, however, well blended with the artistic culture of the Western world, particularly of France. While art critics usually emphasize the Jewish content of Katz' work, it is more in his approach to a subject that the Hasidic character of his work appears — more in the "how" of the painting than the "what." The discriminating observer of Mane Katz' work finds himself in a boldly Hasidic atmosphere saturated with the faith and joy that gave Jewish life its enduring strength — but he will also never fail to find these elements of sophistication and refinement that have placed Katz solidly in the world of twentieth-century art.

Even in works completely devoid of Jewish subject, Katz' Jewish character is vividly present. A noted art-collector browsing through a Katz gallery once stopped suddenly and cried, "Look at that Jewish horse!" And he was right. There were three horses, one black, one white and one pink. They were neighing and seemed about ready to dance but their eyes were sad. Even in his portraiture of animals he could not help but express that strange mixture of lyricism and pathos which is characteristic of the Jewish people.

His great love for color both as a means and as an end is characteristic of his artistic works. In one famous painting, a Jew, completely green against a blue and grey background, plays a recorder

"Saturday Walk in Jerusalem" by Katz

and seems to descend from the heavens with the greatest ease and naturalness. In another picture the same theme is repeated except that the instruments are blue and the Jews playing them yellow and brown. He was a "lyric impressionist," creating a world of joy and sorrow in terms of subtle colors and haunting figures.

Mane Katz had traveled a long way in his artistic career. One of many children born to the beadle of the synagogue in Kremenchug in the Ukraine, he always wanted to be a painter. He went

"Wild Horses" by Katz

A band of musicians by Katz

to Kiev where he ran into good luck: a rich Jew encouraged him and provided him with enough money to travel to Paris, the capital of art. The road to becoming an artist was not an easy one, but

Katz was fired with passion to represent a way of life and individuals in artistic form. Eventually, he succeeded in communicating his vision to the world in enduring art forms.

"I held my first exhibition in Charkov in 1916," he related. "I was twenty-two. When the reviews were printed I couldn't believe my eyes — there was my name in a newspaper, my name! I read the review until I knew it by heart. My work evidently made some impression because I was appointed a Professor of Art in Charkov, and was even given the title of Honorary Doctor. I was very young and short and no one believed I was the professor. Nor did I. This did not last for long because the city was invaded and taken over. I left, moving to Moscow, Minsk, Warsaw, and in November, 1921, to the starting gate for artists: Paris.

"I lived in a very small room and I drew very large pictures. More than once I had to take out the closet and all the furniture in order to be able to see the picture from the proper distance. Those were hard days, but good ones."

Mane Katz succeeded in accomplishing his ambitions and gaining the attention of the world. He was made a Knight of the French Legion of Honor, his painting of the Western Wall won him a gold medal in the Paris 1937 international exhibition. Mane Katz was both a painter and a Jew, and both inseparable elements of his character are inextricably combined in the art with which he has enriched the world.

MAX LIEBERMANN
1847-1935

Max Liebermann's distinguished achievements, along with Israels' and Pissarro's, are among the most important made by Jewish artists in the 19th century. Liebermann's art appeals to that which is in man. He depicts for us ordinary people — peasants and the working class — and the simplest aspects of life.

The Liebermann family belonged to the wealthy class and they disapproved of Max's inclination to devote himself to art. This was especially so because of his "lowly" subject matter. The painter lived a quiet, provincial life but from the moment he chose art as his life's goal, his work became his entire world.

Success did not come easily to him; he struggled hard to achieve the proper effect. In 1873 he painted the *Preserve-Makers* in three different styles and six years later attempted it again. For 13 years he returned to another subject, *Girls Bathing,* no less than 22 times. He painted the same section in the Jewish street in Amsterdam, never repeating it the same way, but always with a new perspective. An art critic tells that he visited Liebermann after the artist had reached his 80th birthday and saw about 25 oil paintings, all depicting a coat lying on a chair. When the artist saw his guest's surprise, he commented: "Do you see how you have to sweat until you get the desired result? I am still not satisfied, although I shall reach my goal..." So severe was his self-discipline.

Liebermann was constantly entering new areas and initiating new ideas in his work. He was the greatest of Jewish painters in Germany and leader of the impressionist movement there. Not only was he an artist, but a man of great character and vitality as well — a devoted German and loyal Jew. He was to become an important figure in public life in Germany. After he had met with success in Paris, in the 1880's, the doors of the National Gallery in Berlin opened to him. For his big exhibition here a special hall was put at his disposal and he was even awarded a gold medal. He was then 40 years old.

In 1898 he was elected to the Academy of Art and awarded the degree of professor. Yet he felt a new institution was needed

"The Seamstress" by Liebermann

to enable artists such as himself to influence the development and direction of German art in accordance with their new spirit and vision. Liebermann therefore joined with some rebel artists at the beginning of the 20th century and formed "Der Berlin Sezession" group which elected him their president. The new group was not a large one, but it succeeded in obtaining key positions in the art world within a short time. The "Sezession" gave Liebermann the vantage point he needed to tear down the walls separating German art from art in other areas of the world. He wanted to give Germany international standards, for then the German artist who could not withstand this test would no longer be admired. These men had built this division, in order to protect their influence and power. The struggle between Liebermann and his rivals reached the court of the Kaiser but Liebermann's enemies, who occupied official positions and wished to keep them at any price, prevented official recognition of "Sezession".

However, artists like Corinth and Slevogt developed, who ultimately assured the success of the "Sezession".

The Academy of Art elected Liebermann as president 20 years after the formation of the "Sezession". Although the term of office is usually one year, so greatly was he respected that he held this position for eight years, until 1928. Afterwards, he held the position of honorary president of the Academy and honorary citizen of Berlin for five years, until the Nazis rose to power.

Liebermann believed that the Academy should involve itself with all good art, without considering any direction in particular. The "Sezession" program ultimately became the program of the Academy itself. The revolutionary Liebermann finally achieved his goals, thus raising the level of art in Germany.

EPHRAIM MOSHE LILIEN
1874-1925

Ephraim Lilien traveled from a small town in Galicia to the art academy in Vienna to fulfill his dream of studying art. A harsh regime was then in power in Austria and Lilien had a difficult time adjusting to its authoritarian character. He disliked a government which restricted the people's freedom, and sought a way to assert his independence. He found it in his art. Some of Lilien's illustrations were published in the magazine *Jugend* (Youth), and from then on he received many orders for drawings from the Bavarian press. The editors wanted only black and white drawings suitable for publication, but by limiting himself to pen and ink, Lilien learned a great deal about this technique.

The art of illustrating books had been neglected during the 19th century; many artists considered it a very unsatisfactory form. Lilien was able to broaden its appeal. He combined the skills of the artist with those of the craftsman and drew highly stylized illustrations that were delicate and yet richly ornamental. He perfected his drawing of the human anatomy and was also expert in depicting plants.

Lilien's special skill and interest lay in drawing anything connected with Judaism — be it the Old Testament, life in the Diaspora, or modern Zionism. He firmly believed in the Zionist cause; it gave him, he said, "a sense of inner freedom." Among his unforgettable drawings is one created especially for the Fifth Zionist Congress, "And Your Eyes Will Be Strengthened When You Go Back to Zion." An aged Jew stands leaning on his cane, beside him an angel with the Star of David on his chest. The angel's hand is on the old Jew's shoulder, and his other hand points to a farmer plowing the earth. The angel appears to be pointing the way to Zion, the land of Israel. The picture was reprinted in hundreds of newspapers during the Congress and it hangs on the walls of thousands of homes.

Lilien's crowning work was his illustration of the Bible. Before he began this monumental task, the artist traveled to Palestine to obtain first-hand knowledge of the background for the people and events he would portray. Lilien himself handled all of the details for this project, choosing special paper, selecting the most suitable type designs, establishing the layout and design of the volume, and even determining the type of binding. Another labor of love was teaching at the Bezalel Art School in Jerusalem, where he had been invited to serve as an art instructor.

Ephraim Lilien is an outstanding example of a man who combined professional talent with personal belief, using one to enhance the other. His interest in and devotion to Judaism served as his special inspiration and his artistic talents enabled him to help the cause of Zionism in his own unique way.

Lilien often depicted the sad plight of the wandering Jew

Lilien's son, by the artist

JACQUES (CHAIM JACOB) LIPCHITZ
1891-

Jacques Lipchitz is considered by many European and American art critics to rank among the two or three greatest sculptors in the world. Sir Herbert Read placed him on a level with Henry Moore, Brancusi and Giacometti, adding: "From the beginning of the cubist period until today, Jacques Lipchitz has remained one of our foremost sculptors. He has altered and expanded our entire conception of bronze casting." A Dutch critic wrote, "One is reminded of Rodin and even Michelangelo when one considers his experience and knowledge." Swiss critics have acclaimed him "the greatest cubist sculptor." Lipchitz himself maintains: "What particularly characterizes me is the search for new paths."

Lipchitz has always been one of the foremost innovators in sculpture, starting new trends which others have followed. In his youth he was friendly with Picasso, and due to the latter's influence turned to cubism. He was the first to see the mathematical, geometrically-based structure of forms, and therefore he is for many the greatest of the abstract sculptors. A huge statue by Lipchitz, called the *Spirit of Innovation*, shows a pioneer looking into the distance, guided by an eagle. It stands in a Philadelphia park.

Lipchitz realizes that for many, his sculpture seems crude and strange, expressive but not beautiful. "Everyone knows that I know what is beautiful and harmonious," he explains, "but I am too old to be concerned about these things... I create sacrifices in order to expand that art which we call sculpture."

The famous French patron of modern art, Father M. A. Couturier, commissioned Lipchitz to create a sculpture of Mary and Jesus for his church in Assas. Lipchitz' first reaction was: "Don't you know that I am a Jew?" Father Couturier, a Dominican priest, replied, "If that fact doesn't disturb you it won't disturb me." When he had finished his work Lipchitz signed the sculpture with his fingerprints, adding: "Jacob Lipchitz, Jew, faithful to the religion of his fathers, made this Virgin for the sake of better understanding between men on earth and in order that the spirit of man will reign supreme."

"The 'Kapparot' Sacrifice" by Lipchitz

At a time when he was working on many commissions Lipchitz suffered a violent emotional shock, which would have stopped many others from working. On the night of January 5, 1952, his studio, containing the models of most of his works, went up in flames, destroying his private collection of modern French art and primitive sculpture. "A part of my life has been destroyed," he mourned. "I will have to begin everything anew." From memory, Lipchitz began to reconstruct his sculptures and ordered a new studio, overlooking the Hudson River.

Among Lipchitz' works are several variations on the theme, *Man Playing a Musical Instrument*. This subject occupied him for fifteen years, during which time he cast this figure innumerable times, until he achieved his aim — the seeming disappearance of the man and the musical instrument, so that the sculpture embodied the art of playing itself. *Prometheus* is another of Lipchitz' favorite subjects, although his conception of it has changed with the passage of time During World War II Lipchitz' Prometheus epitomized the struggle for survival, while another Prometheus, created after the Nazi defeat, is represented as victorious. In another of Lipchitz' sculptures the figure of the cockerel constitutes a recurring theme. These statues represent "atonement," a subject which has fascinated him from both the human and philosophical aspects, and in which he has found a symbolic expression of his Jewishness.

Most of his sculptures, however, have no simple explanation; they must be experienced personally. As a critic wrote: "The test of an abstract sculpture is that although the observer does not understand it he feels that it would have been impossible to create it any differently."

When Lipchitz arrived in Paris at the age of 18 from his birthplace in Lithuania, he developed a liking for Greek sculpture. His first works received praise from the elderly Rodin. Subsequently the Mexican painter, Diego Rivera, took him to Montmartre and introduced him to Picasso. He was friendly with the painter Juan Gris and the writer and art connoisseur, Gertrude Stein. He was

"The Rape of Europa" by Lipchitz

practically penniless until he finally received recognition, at a time when he was nine months in arrears with his rent. An American art collector, Dr. Albert Barnes, visited Lipchitz' studio and purchased eight stone sculptures, ordering an additional five.

As time passed, his sculptures took on new forms. His attempts to find a new abstract language reached their peak in his famous work, *Form*. After this period Lipchitz returned to Greek mythology and the Old Testament as sources of inspiration and created many wonderful works using these themes. As a result of this trend in his work he created his greatest sculpture, over 30 feet high,

Prometheus Strangling the Hawk, for the World Exhibition held in Paris in 1937. With the fall of France in World War II Lipchitz deserted his studio in Paris and established himself in New York. As an expression of his emotions on the slaughter in Europe, Lipchitz created one of his most powerful works, *Mother and Child.* It shows a woman without legs, her arms raised, with a child holding onto her neck.

A visit to France at the end of the war made him realize that he was neither American nor French, but Jewish. Lipchitz returned to the United States with a commission for a work in honor of the new State of Israel. When Israel was established in 1948 he created an outstanding sculpture, *The Miracle* — a man in the form of the two tablets of the Law, with arms raised high, resembling the seven-branched candelabra. Lipchitz' Jewishness comes through in many of his works. As he himself once said: "Even when I cast the figure of Prometheus, it is a Jewish Prometheus."

AMADEO MODIGLIANI
1884-1920

The room was small, stale-smelling, messy. Piles of paintings stood in the corners, a palette and a few cups still containing coffee dregs cluttered a kitchen table. A broken chair and an iron bed, its grey bedclothes twisted in a heap in the middle, completed the furnishings. Someone slept and worked here, but it wasn't a home.

He flung the still-wet painting into a corner. Once again, a failure! It wasn't what he wanted. For years he had been in Paris, twelve years. Worthwhile, successful artists lived all around him. He worked as seriously and as hard as they did but he felt that his work was weak, empty. He coughed. There was a knock at the door.

"Monsieur Modigliani, the rent. It has been two months." "I'll pay you by the end of the week." He had another fit of coughing.

"You had better pay me... why don't you see a doctor, Monsieur. Very well, by the end of the week."

As soon as the door was locked and the coughing attack had stopped, "Modi" began to tie his paintings in bundles. Time to move again! He would stay with Raoul for a while perhaps. At least he might eat properly. If only he could talk Raoul or someone into lending him tools and stone. Maybe he wasn't meant to be a painter, but he *knew* he could sculpt. If only.

Modigliani died when he was thirty-five years old of tuberculosis, just another foreigner in Paris. A complete failure, he had no home and lived on his friends' charity. His was a typical bohemian life in early twentieth-century Paris, friends, parties, drinking, working and starving, poverty, cold rooms, shabby clothing. No wonder he broke down under the strain.

There had been only one Modigliani exhibition in all the years he had worked there. The only picture sold was brought back the next day because the buyer's wife thought it too ugly for her pretty parlor. One day, someone had glanced through the window and seeing that some of the portraits were of people unclothed, had informed the police, which sent a policeman to tell the gallery

Modigliani's slender women are characterized by long, clean lines and elongated features

"Mario" by Modigliani

Modigliani self-portrait

"The Bohemienne" by Modigliani

'nja Czechowska' by Modigliani

owner she would have to remove the nudes. This was the only attention the exhibition received.

What a short wasted life! He burned himself out, never knowing that he was one of the greatest painters of the twentieth century. If only he could have sold one of his works, just one, at today's prices, he could have lived well and worked on to a normal old age. When one of his paintings is up for sale today it is an event that brings buyers from all over the world. The bidding starts at 200,000 francs. Modigliani had not been able to sell any of his paintings, even at 200 francs. He never had enough money for canvas or oils, and certainly not enough for his dreamed-of sculpting materials.

A portrait by Modigliani is stamped through and through with his own unmistakable style. Each one is part of his own unique world, brothers and sisters to each other. Yet each of his portraits is a unique person, with his own individual character and expression. Each has a long, thin neck, an oval head, tight lips. The body flows from the head, the shoulders slope, all with incredible grace. Every portrait — usually only the upper half of the body — has its own warm colors, and each color stands out.

His portraits make you think of landscapes and still lifes, although they are really paintings of people. The person seems to be part of a scene, the way a flower or tree is part of a scene, fitting into it, and yet standing out.

Modigliani came from an old, well-known Italian Jewish family. When he met someone he would say, "I'm Modigliani, the Jew." He faced anti-Semitism squarely, and would never allow an insult to pass. He remembered how his grandfather had been forced to sell back a piece of land he had bought near Rome, because of the law forbidding Jews to own land in Italy. His mother had often told him about his famous ancestor, Spinoza, the philosopher, and he was proud of this heritage, as well as of his father's banking family.

Modigliani spent his life trying to find himself and to express his vision of the world. In the attempt he created a world of beauty and magic for those who lived after him, if not for himself.

MORITZ OPPENHEIM
1800-1882

The young man arrived at the life-class and sat down some distance from the nude model. Because he could not see clearly he moved closer. The teacher walked over to the young man and said mockingly, "Why do you sit so close? You draw only Jews."

The professor was completely right. The young Jew, Moritz Oppenheim; did indeed draw only Jews. Many other artists also specialized in Jewish subjects both before and after Oppenheim but none could equal his paintings of Jewish life. Typical Jewish themes inspired such paintings as *Havdalla* (1865), *Sabbath Afternoon* (1866), *Sabbath Night* (1867).

Moritz Oppenheim was the first Jewish painter to make a name for himself after the gates of the Eastern European ghettos were thrown open by Napoleon's armies, which happened when he was a boy of eleven. He was the first Jewish student to enter an art academy, where he spent his time copying from the antique casts of famous sculptures of the Greek and Roman classic period and the Renaissance. He showed such talent that his parents decided to send him to Munich which was famous as a city of art and artists.

But Munich did not satisfy the young painter for long. At the age of twenty, he set off for the true Mecca of art: Paris. There he worked hard, improving his technique and absorbing everything around him. But he longed to go on and to see another great capital and art center. He appealed to Baron James de Rothschild, who agreed that Oppenheim could accompany one of his agents on his next journey to Italy.

In Rome Moritz entered some of his work in a competition at St. Luke's Academy of Painting; the judges found his entry worthy of a prize, but as a Jew he could not receive the award.

All his life Moritz Oppenheim remained an Orthodox Jew, strictly observing kashrut and keeping all festivals and fasts. For his

"The Wedding" by Oppenheim

paintings he chose such themes as *Abraham and his Family, The Sacrifice of Isaac, Jacob's Blessing.* Although his religion made success in his profession difficult, for the Church exerted a great influence on art, Oppenheim's work had much in common with these Church-inspired paintings. Both shared a preoccupation with the glories of the past and a determination to preserve in paint a world which had vanished.

Many art lovers, appreciating Oppenheim's talent, tried to induce him to abandon the faith of his fathers, but they only succeeded in making him more deeply attached to his religion. He contrasted the noble simplicity of their synagogue with the superficial splendor of the Church which, in his eyes, was only for display. "Our dim houses of prayer elevate my soul and spirit and, in my eyes, they are lofty and sanctified..." he wrote in his journal.

Oppenheim's friendship with the Rothschild family was of great help to him. They encouraged him with sincere admiration, bought his paintings and smoothed his path wherever he was. He lived in Naples for some years, although Jews were forbidden to live there and he had difficulty in finding a *minyan* to say *kaddish* after his mother's death. After five years in France, Oppenheim returned to Frankfurt — by now a famous man.

There were few outstanding painters in Germany at this time and his reputation increased. Important people flocked to his studio, ordering portraits for which they paid him handsomely. He became so famous that the Munich Museum awarded him an honorary diploma — the first time a Jew was so honored.

He was considered unequalled in his profession of portraiture. Whether his subjects were beautiful women, men of the world, or "character" studies, all Oppenheim's portraits displayed the artist's acute psychological insight and masterly technique.

Oppenheim at work

Today we would find his works perhaps "over-sweet," his subjects idealized. His importance as a painter of the Jewish life has, however, stood the test of time. He was a faithful reporter of people, customs and incidents of the Jewish scene of his generation. Throughout his long life, Oppenheim remained an upright Jew, bringing honor to his people and, through his art, leaving an imperishable legacy.

CHANA ORLOFF
1888- 1968

A sculptress to compare with the great Rodin ? Impossible, the reader may be inclined to say. Sculpting involves slaving over marble, bronze and wood, forging them into works of art. Even men have difficulty at times working with the sculpting materials. Strange as it may seem, Chana Orloff has been praised by experts and artists as one of the finest sculptors of her day.

Chana's had been one of five Jewish families living in the small Ukrainian village of Tsare-Constantinovska, where Russian pogroms hit often and life was unbearably hard. Their house was down at least once, her father found work difficult, if not impossible, to find. Finally, the family moved to Palestine in 1905, and six years later decided that Chana should become a seamstress. She was then sent to the fashion center of the world, Paris, where she began her studies at the Ecole des Arts Decoratifs (School of Decorative Arts).

Originally, the family's plan had been for her to remain in Paris only for two or three weeks to learn the essentials of her trade. "But," she said, "when I stepped out of the Gare de Lyon railway station and breathed that special air of the capital of the world, I felt I just had to stay more than two weeks." She remained there more than fifty years.

It was quite by accident that Chana turned to sculpture. A friend of hers, a Russian student, asked her one morning if she would like to watch a sculptor do his portrait. Chana agreed and went to the studio. There, the sculptor worked busily, throwing his arms about wildly, breathing hard, and giving every indication of a man struggling desperately with impossible work.

Chana could not control herself and burst out laughing at the grotesque show. The artist was, of course, highly insulted, and demanded to know if *she* could do any better. "Give me the materials and I'll try," was her answer. The sculptor threw down the plaster and chisel in anger and stalked out of the room. Her friend was aghast. "Did you ever study sculpting?" he asked in agitation. "No," she said, "but it looks easy enough."

By afternoon, she had completed a bust of the angry sculptor

"Girl Playing with a Ball" by Chana Orloff

from memory. When he saw the work, he became furious and began shouting angrily, "You lied! You have indeed learned sculpting!"

That night, a few visitors — artists all — came to the studio. After seeing the sculpture and listening to the remarkable story behind it, they all agreed that Chana was in the wrong field. "You must learn art and become a sculptress," they said. Chana agreed, and thus was started on her career.

In 1913, Chana had her first exhibition at the Galerie d'Automne. Eleven years later her work was exhibited with that of two other artists, Roualt and Matisse, at the Galerie Bernheim. Chana was on the road to success.

For years, she worked in her studio in Paris, the art capital of the world, and became widely known in art circles there. Her sculptures in iron, bronze, marble and wood were highly acclaimed and exhibited in galleries from the United States to Israel.

What was it that made her work so striking, so exceptional? It certainly was not vivid likeness to her subjects, as even her portraits often lacked any obvious similarities to their subjects. Chana was sensitive to a subject's character and would simplify and exaggerate his most salient features, thus capturing the true essence of his personality. She instilled inanimate materials with humor and a love of life. There was freshness, subtlety and even mystery in her work that attracted viewers a second and third time. Despite their deviation from reality, her works are almost more alive than life itself, a factor which helped to elevate Chana to the rank of unquestioned greatness. She has been cited as one of the best of the modern sculptors, and without a doubt one of the foremost women artists of all time.

CAMILLE PISSARRO
1830-1903

Compared to the work of other Impressionists such as Renoir, Monet and Degas, the paintings of Camille Pissarro are perhaps somewhat difficult to appreciate, with their intellectual rather than emotional appeal. But it was Camille Pissarro who had the greatest influence on all other Impressionist painters, and the one who gave the movement the most meaning. For this leading role, Pissarro is called the "Father of Impressionism."

The Impressionist painters used the laws of optics, the science of light, to create their "impression" of what they were painting. They did not seek to portray what they saw in a realistic way. Instead, they filtered the image through their own awareness, feelings and sensitivities.

Born in the Virgin Islands of a Jewish father and a Creole mother, Pissarro received his education in Paris. Returning to the Islands, he helped his father in his store, but already showed a talent and preference for painting. Camille begged to be allowed to go to art school, but his father refused, arguing that the life of the artist is usually a difficult one. This verbal struggle continued

Like so many of his contemporaries, Pissarro found the geometric patterns in bridges a fascinating challenge

Pissarro at the easel

for five years, until Pissarro finally ran away to Venezuela. In 1855, Pissarro arrived in Paris and entered the world of art. Like many young artists, Pissarro found his new life difficult, and there were moments when the poor student wondered if his father might not have been right after all.

Pissarro would take his easel out into the open air and paint in the street and the field, using light brush strokes to produce a spontaneous rendering of leaves and flowers, and especially of the

"Isle of Lacroix, Rouen" by Pissarro

play of light and shadow. In his paintings, one finds subtle colors blended with pleasing harmony. He rarely painted portraits of people, as few commissions came his way. However, Pissarro did leave four self-portraits.

In his first paintings, one can see the influence of the great painter, Jean Corot. Although he learned much from the latter, especially with regard to abstract forms, Pissarro always maintained an independent style of painting. In a letter to his son, Lucien,

Pissarro's "Hermitage at Pointoise"

"A Street in Pontoise" by Pissarro

Pissarro wrote that uniqueness does not reside in the subject of the painting, but rather in the form of expression given to it by the artist. He also complained that the middle class cared only for silly sentiment in art, and had lost all taste for beauty. Therefore a new movement was needed. Pissarro was to become the leader of this movement.

When all three paintings he submitted for the annual exhibition at the "Salon" were rejected by the judges, the affair attained so much publicity that it reached the attention of the Emperor himself. Napoleon III examined the paintings which had caused such controversy — they included paintings by Monet, Renoir, Cezanne and Degas as well as those of Pissarro — and demanded their inclusion. He suggested the creation of a special salon so that the world would be able to judge the new art movement for itself. Thus, in 1874, the "Salon of the Rejected" was established.

Although many people came to the exhibits at the "Salon of the Rejected," the paintings were at first regarded as "pop art" is today. People felt that these works, with their bright colors and free lines were original and daring, but hardly enduring. However, Pissarro's lasting reputation and the popularity that his pictures enjoy today have shown these predictions to be wrong and the impact of the Impressionist school cannot be denied.

REUVEN RUBIN
1893-

One of fourteen children of the Zelikowitch family in the Galacz Ghetto in Rumania, Reuven was so talented that he won first prize for the best elementary school graduate in the country. As a sign of honor and merit a paper crown was placed on his head inscribed with the name of the crown prince, Carol. Naturally, the talented boy wished to continue his studies at the gymnasium, if he could do this free of charge. But there was one problem, endorsements of three non-Jews were required to testify to his worthiness. Where could three such signatures be found in a land that was traditionally anti-Semitic?

Thus, at 13, the boy set out on his first diplomatic mission: to find three votes. The police officer at the Galacz Ghetto, who was well acquainted with the family, was the first. A second came from a grocer. But from where would the third signature come? Reuven was told about a good-hearted, rich man who lived beyond the ghetto walls who did much to help people, including Jews. With the petition in his hand, Reuven entered the rich man's mansion when a tremendous Alsatian dog jumped on him, bit him until he bled and knocked him to the ground. He fainted, and when he regained consciousness he was lying in his bed at home with his wounds bandaged, the precious piece of paper still in his hand but with the coveted signature on it. Thus, the doors of the gymnasium were opened to Reuven.

Reuven was 18 when he left the Rumanian ghetto from which he had absorbed so much Jewish folklore, Jewish customs and Jewish hopes, and set out on the long road to Eretz Israel with nothing in his pouch but his hopes. Here Reuven dedicated himself to painting and capturing the spiritual life of his people and land on canvas. For 38 years he worked unceasingly until he won his place as the foremost representative artist of the ancient land which had at last reverted to the Jewish people. Through his painting he helped transmit the cultural heritage of the Jews to the world.

In 1948, appointed first ambassador of the State of Israel to Rumania, he returned to his birthplace in order to help create material

Rubin's subjects "force me to reveal themselves"

and spiritual ties between the two countries. For a year and a half, he filled this important post. After that, however, he returned to his brush. Eighteen months was too long to be away from his beloved painting, which he felt was as important to his nation's destiny as his political career.

In 1924, he held his first exhibition in Migdal David, the famous Tower of David, in Jerusalem, and in 1932 in the Tel Aviv Museum and his works have since been shown in more than a hundred exhibitions, forty of them in America. In 1923 he issued an album of woodcuts, *The Seekers of God*. He has also painted stage sets and designed costumes for 16 plays of the Habima and Ohel theaters. Meanwhile, his fame spread across the world and it was he who brought the traditional spiritual treasures of the Jews to world knowledge. Two generations took pleasure in his pictures, his olive groves, the views of Jaffa and Jerusalem, Safed and the Kinneret, the figures of farmers and pioneers. Haim Nachman Bialik described Rubin's work as "a collection of legends, the legend of Eretz Israel."

Rubin was the moving spirit of a small group of young artists who did not find satisfaction in the conservative atmosphere of previous painters and who aspired to a new art which would be deeply rooted in the homeland and in the life of the young country. Together with his friends, he helped to organize the historic exhibition in Jerusalem in 1924, which today is considered the point of departure of the new art in the country.

Sometimes called "the Paul Gauguin of Israel," Rubin's characteristics are his moral vision, his simple, noble humanity, and his love of his people and his land. He will never paint anything that he does not love or deeply believe in. "I do not choose the style or the subject," the artist once said, "They force me to reveal themselves. I paint from the approach of an artist who does not agree to any hint of artistic subjection but together with this is alive to the life around him."

BORIS (ZALMAN DOV) SCHATZ
1866-1932

In 1875 an emissary from Palestine came to Rovno, Latvia, and related in the synagogue the wonders of the Holy Land: the Wailing Wall, Rachel's tomb, and the other monuments of Israel's glorious past. Boris Schatz, a 9-year-old boy in the congregation, listened eagerly to the words of the emissary and then implored his father to take him to the hotel where the man was staying so that he could look at the pictures of the holy places which he had brought with him. The pictures, however, did not satisfy the boy. He vowed that when he was older he would study art and go to Palestine and draw the holy monuments properly. While in the emissary's room, he was entranced by the representation of Bezalel ben Uri, the first Biblical craftsman, artist and builder of the Tabernacle in the desert. The young Schatz decided that he himself would renew the ancient tradition of Israel's art and found an art academy in the Holy Land.

In 1906 Schatz realized his youthful dream when he immigrated to Palestine. He had given up an important position as court sculptor of Bulgaria and director of the Museum and Academy of Visual Art in the capital city of Sofia in order to found in Jerusalem an academy of arts and crafts, which he called the Bezalel School. Not only did this school have traditional art classes but also workshops where the students did work in copper, silver filigree, wood, stone and rug weaving. Schatz also established a national museum. He sent letters to Jewish philanthropists all over the world, appealing to them to donate works of art to the museum which he established in association with the art school. From this beginning grew the Bezalel Museum, with its large and varied collection of Jewish ritual art.

Boris Schatz was both enthusiastic and optimistic. He was the first Jewish artist who attempted to create a characteristic, national Jewish art, free from foreign influence, and his abundant energy and boundless dedication to the cause of modern Jewish art assured him a place of honor in its history. Although he had worked in Bulgaria for ten years, it was in Palestine that he found his true

calling. Here he produced his lovely reliefs, among them, *The Blessing of the Candles, The Penitent, A Portion of My Labor, The Wailing Wall on the Ninth of Ab, The Matchmaker* and *Havdalah*. In addition to these reliefs, he painted portraits of many famous Jews, including Zionist leaders Theodor Herzl, Max Nordau and David Wolfson, sculptor Mark Antokolsky, composer Anton Rubinstein, and many others. He also painted Biblical figures, such as Jeremiah, Deborah, King David, Judith and Mattathias the Hasmonean. Schatz's art, however, was overshadowed by his most important project: the founding and direction of the Bezalel School for Arts and Crafts.

The Bezalel School quickly developed into a double enterprise: the workshops and school on the one hand, and the museum on the other. Bezalel must be viewed in the light of recent Jewish history. During the cultural renaissance of the Jews since the end of the 1800's, and particularly at the beginning of the present century, several pioneering enterprises were founded in Palestine by the young Zionist movement. But it was Bezalel, founded by Boris Schatz,which gained the greatest publicity and recognition throughout the world. Everything which came forth from Palestine appealed to the hearts of the Jews in the Diaspora: the resurrection of the Hebrew language, the immigration of working youth as pioneers, the wines, and other innovations. But the creation of a new national Hebrew art affected the people most of all. The exhibition of Bezalel works which was organized in Odessa in 1910 by the committee of the pioneering "Lovers of Zion" (Hovevei Zion) aroused tremendous enthusiasm. Although the work of the Bezalel artists at that time could not compete on a professional level with world art, the fact that it was produced in Palestine captured the hearts of the Jewish viewers. This was the secret of its charm and attraction.

"A national art," Professor Shatz once said, "is an art which comes from the heart and works in harmony with the heart of the nation". He brought to his institution teachers with the same convictions as his own. These included Ephraim Lilien, Samuel

"The first Commandment" by Schatz

Hirszenberg and Abel Pann. Their students were youngsters from all over the world, who later became famous as producers of a Palestinian style of art. Although the artistic level of the teachers and students ultimately became very high, the primary consideration, to produce a national art and to revive the ancient humanitarian spirit of the Hebrew people through its art, was never lost sight of. Today we can witness the flowering of art in Israel. Most of the artists working there today are graduates of Bezalel. The late sculptor Ben Zvi, and the painters Nahum Gutmann, Reuven Rubin, Hannah Ticho and Pinchas Litvinovsky as well as many others, received their training at Bezalel.

The initiative of Professor Schatz knew no bounds. He helped to develop different branches of arts and crafts, thereby providing a livelihood for many people. He not only found markets for the products of hundreds of stone workers and rug weavers, but obtained land in Ben-Shemen through the Jewish National Fund and established a village of Yemenite craftsmen, thereby blending agriculture and crafts. He regarded a workshop as a practical tool by which to transform groups of unemployed people into productive wage earners. In addition to painting and sculpture, this school taught dyeing, spinning and carpet weaving. Domestic crafts were encouraged as a source of work for young girls and old women in the towns and villages.

The Bezalel Museum contains treasures of Jewish and general art of every form, ancient and modern, as well as a library numbering thousands of volumes. It has become a truly national museum, just as the Bezalel school has grown into the national school for arts and crafts. Professor Schatz's dream of founding an art academy has been realized. He is the recognized father of the renewal of art in Israel.

BEN SHAHN
1898-

Not by chance is the 1951 biography of Shahn called *Portrait of the Artist as an American*. Although he was born in Kovno, Russia, and brought to America at the age of eight, he is considered more American in his subject matter than most native artists. In the 1954 Venice Biennale, Shahn was one of the two artists chosen by the Museum of Modern Art to represent the United States, a year in which he also won a prize at the Sao Paulo Museum in Brazil. The critic James Sobey evaluates Shahn's contribution to contemporary art thus: "He is one of the authentic and strongest American humanists, an artist, translating the American subject to a brilliant personal declaration of unification with humanity."

The goal Shahn had set himself at an early age was to describe America by means of his brush, with special emphasis on social conditions. He loves to tell stories in his works, and feels that art must be total, that is, theme, composition, color, craft must all receive equal attention from the artist, although choice of subject has generally proven most important for him. In most cases, and because of his inclination to tell a story, he does not limit himself to one picture on the subject, but prepares a complete series of paintings or drawings devoted to the same theme. In 1932, he did a series of 23 satiric gouaches on the scandalous Sacco and Vanzetti trial, the two Italians accused of the murder of a night-watchman and convicted, according to many, for cynical political reasons. This was just the kind of social theme that Shahn was most attracted to.

In 1940, 375 artists entered a competition for a mural decoration for the Social Security Building in Washington. Shahn won and created an intensely moving work. A boy on crutches, two small girls looking with horror at an accident, a despairing family whose father had been killed in a work-accident — each of his pictures in this mural revealed a story and raised a social issue. *Death of a Miner* (1947) revealed the hazardous conditions under which many laborers worked.

Shahn had deep Jewish roots. He has always had particular interest in anything pertaining to Judaism and its problems. Between

1930 and 1935 he completed a series of paintings on the Passover Haggadah and the book of Ecclesiastes and was always deeply fascinated by the twenty-two letters of the Hebrew alphabet.

One can trace his deep concern for social justice to his childhood. When Shahn was 6 years old, his father, a carpenter and wood-carver by profession, was arrested for socialist activities and deported. He succeeded in reaching South Africa, and several years later he got to America and sent for his wife and three children. No wonder that, given this family background, Shahn shares Blake's thought that protest against injustice is the true adoration of God.

Shahn was once asked to lecture on Jewish art. He began by saying that this does not exist. There are Jewish artists and Jewish subjects, but there is no Jewish art. "If this is to be, Israel must be isolated from the rest of the world for a long time." The important thing in Shahn's eyes is not to stand aside and be apathetic to what is going on, but to be involved with what is going on, to draw people into a closer awareness of the role they play in the world around them. If involvement is the responsibility of each individual and the Jewish artist in particular, Shahn has indeed fulfilled his obligation.

CHAIM SOUTINE
1894-1943

Soutine by Modigliani

Chaim Soutine, like his paintings, was the picture of despair. His hair curled wildly about his homely, scarred face, and his red nose rested absurdly above a thick, sad mouth. Even in his early days in Paris, he was so bent over that he appeared to be almost a hunchback. So filthy and unkempt was he that the Russian sculptor Metchnikoff, who boarded him in his room, claimed that he had to set up a moat to separate his bed from Soutine's. "I did this," he said, "because I didn't want his germs coming over to me!"

Soutine had come to France in 1913 as a poor refugee from an obscure village in Lithuania. But the village haunted him even in golden Paris. The trees he painted in France look as if they have been uprooted; the houses are grotesque and tormented; the backgrounds twist and turn as though in flames. Even his flowers look like wounds dripping blood. "He seems to be drawing on a kitchen towel," someone once said to M. George Michel, noted commentator on the bohemian life of that period. "Perhaps," Michel replied, "but he lights a grand hellfire."

Slaughtered animals were favorite themes of Chaim Soutine. As in his landscapes and portraits, the canvas seems to bespeak imminent catastrophe, of life bordering on death. His slaughtered rabbit appears to be still twitching in apprehension; his dead and plucked chicken remains open-beaked with terror.

Despite his strange appearance and his even stranger subject matter, Soutine began to attract admirers. "He draws meat in fantastic colors, the likes of which you haven't seen since Rembrandt," exclaimed the poet Zaborovsky, who decided to help Soutine achieve recognition. He tried to get Soutine to dress properly, but the artist declared, "That is impossible. I cannot dress like the Kaiser every day." George Michel also set out to help Soutine and finally persuaded an influential art dealer to display one of his works. It was purchased by Dr. Bernes, prominent owner of the richest col-

Soutine's "Girl in Blue"

"Dogs and Forks" by Soutine

Self-portrait by Soutine

lection of modern paintings at that time. Bernes later brought more Soutines from Zaborovsky, sometimes paying 70,000 francs for them.

Thus began Soutine's golden period. Bernes presented the artist with a gift of a beautiful villa in southern France, and the once slovenly bohemian now walked the streets like a lord.

But Soutine's old ways and old despair soon returned. He burned many of his canvasses, but his work was in such demand that he was paid 12,000 francs in 1920 for a fragment of one of these destroyed works. He began to revert to his former careless ways of dress and Michel relates that the last time he saw Soutine the artist was in the marketplace looking for a chicken to paint. He wanted a thin chicken with a long neck. The shopkeeper thought he was dealing with a poor laborer and from pity held up a fat chicken and said, "Don't worry. For the same price I'll give you this one."

Soutine bought a small apartment in the Montmartre, and took in many poor Jewish refugees. Checks for large sums of money from all over the world were always lying about, but he was negligent about going to banks to cash them. He had only 23 francs in his pocket when he died, from exhaustion, during the German occupation in 1943.

One of Soutine's last paintings was sold for a million francs. His works have been exhibited at the Venice Biennial and the Louvre has a room set aside for his paintings. Although Soutine never pursued success and recognition, it came to him almost unbidden, a tribute to the strange artist who saw and portrayed beauty in the distorted and the grotesque.

JACOB STEINHARDT
1887-1968

"Dear Mr. Liebermann: The young man who brings this letter to you has some drawings to show you. Please give us your honest professional opinion of his talents..." The artist folded the letter and sighed wearily.

The boy held his breath as he watched the noted artist, Max Liebermann, take up his drawings. Then his heart sank as he saw the master shake his head, putting down each sketch after a brief glance.

"I'm afraid these aren't good enough to be printed," he murmured. The boy wanted to escape, to tear up the drawings.

"What's this? What's this?" exclaimed the master when he came to one picture. "Here's something — now yes! That's good!" And the young man, who a moment before had wanted to destroy his work, walked out of the master's house into a 60-year career as a distinguished artist.

The boy was Jacob Steinhardt, who at the age of 15 was sent to Berlin to Mr. Liebermann. He had wanted to study art and there were a few rich people in his little home town of Posen, then part of Prussia, who were willing to pay for his lessons, but they wanted first to be sure that he had talent.

The picture that impressed Liebermann was a portrait of Jacob's grandfather. It was not the kind of portrait people usually painted in those days — that of a dignified old man with a big mustache, staring out severely from the canvas. This was a picture of a sick old man, lying in bed with the anguish of old age and dying clearly depicted.

Thus Jacob Steinhardt received Liebermann's recommendation and enough money to study art for seven years. He worked with Corinth, another German Jew, in Paris and with Matisse in Italy. Steinhardt became part of the new wave of German painting after World War I, and although he found himself pulled in different directions by the different schools of painting, he continued to study the classic techniques of composition, etching and wood carving. He and some other young Jewish artists formed the

A woodcut by Steinhardt

Steinhardt at work

"Pathetikar" school of expressionism. It did not get a very good reception from the critics, but young German poets found it inspirational.

During these years Steinhardt took no special interest in Jewish subjects; his general education had been very German, very modern. The turning point came for him in 1917, when as a soldier in the German Army he met for the first time the ghetto Jews of

"Sabbath," woodcut by Steinhardt

Galicia and Latvia. This was the way of life that many Jews had fled from and which outsiders regarded with contempt. But Steinhardt was attracted to it. He began to draw these distant cousins of his, with their rich culture and tradition which made no apologies for being Jewish. He was to continue drawing such people for the rest of his life.

Jacob Steinhardt first visited Palestine in 1925. Jerusalem fascinated him and he drew its walls, its twisting alleys, its market place. In 1933 he settled there permanently.

Steinhardt illustrated the Haggadah (the story of Passover) and characters and scenes from the Bible. His illustrations enriched the works of Peretz, Agnon and Shalom Aleichem. The subject matter was usually Jewish, and although he had worked in watercolors, oils and pastels he became best known for his etchings and woodcuts.

He became director of the Bezalel School of Art in Jerusalem, the city which never lost its charm for him. During the 1950's he received the Holy Art prize at Venice and was judged Best Artist of Jerusalem. Jerusalem is a world of light and shadow, and he set it down that way. The old orthodox Jew slowly moving down a winding alley, as if you could touch him, with the houses jutting sharply over the street — this is Steinhardt's Jerusalem. The old Jew seems to have come out of the Bible — but he is a part of eternal Jerusalem and Jerusalem is part of him.

YOSSI STERN
1923-

If you were to attend a definitive exhibition of Yossi Stern's work, you might, at first, experience some confusion. What exactly is this artist's style? Is he a cartoonist and caricaturist? Is he a realist, a cubist, an impressionist? Is he trying to evoke sympathy, humor, ridicule, anger? Then, as the meaning of Yossi Stern and his work begins to emerge, the confusion vanishes and it is clear that Stern is actually all of these things. Yossi Stern is, in a sense, the embodiment of the spirit of Israel, and especially of its people; he will use any medium, any style, any technique which will enable him to express that spirit in its many facets and moods. But one thing never changes in any of his paintings and drawings—his uncanny ability to capture the ambience of a locale or a situation, the emotion in a face or a human confrontation.

Stern was born in 1923 in the village of Kayar, in the Bakon mountains of Hungary. At the age of ten he moved with his family to Budapest, and in 1939, as the clouds of war gathered over Europe and the Nazi hordes spread eastward, he managed to join a group of young refugees who were setting out on the perilous route to Palestine on a small vessel, the "Zechariah". The ship finally reached Palestine, then under British administration, in early 1940, but Stern and his fellow passengers were arrested by the authorities as illegal immigrants. He was detained in a prison camp for six months.

On his release, he was cared for by Youth Aliyah and the Betar youth organization. He received agricultural training in various villages, working in orange groves, in tobacco fields and on road building. In 1943, thanks to a group of friends and with the assistance of Youth Aliyah, all of whom recognized his early artistic promise, he was given the opportunity to study at Palestine's foremost art institute, The Bezalel Art School in Jerusalem, under Mordecai Ardon. Three years later Yossi Stern graduated, winning the Hermann Struck Award as Outstanding Student, and was immediately engaged by the school as an instructor, a position he still holds.

In 1947 he embarked upon his first major work as an illustrator, in the volume *Menorat Hazahav* ("The Golden Lamp"), by Asher Barash, for which he did the woodcuts. Book illustration continued to be one of his major fields and among the scores of books which he has illustrated are the works of Shakespeare.

In 1947, as Israel's struggle for independence entered its final and decisive phase, Stern became a "war illustrator." He was in Jerusalem throughout the siege of the city as staff artist of the army's Jerusalem

Stern's "Family"

YOSSI STERN

weekly and, after the siege was lifted in the summer of 1948, he joined the staff of the official army weekly, *Bamachane*. That same year the published a highly successful book, *Begius Maleh* ("Total Mobilization"), a selection of sketches of his wartime experience. That year he also held a one-man exhibition in Tel Aviv.

In 1949, on a grant from the Israel Ministry of Education, he went to London to study for a year at the Royal College of Art. He spent the

Stern at work "in the field"

An example of Stern's technique of combining abstraction and realism

following year painting and studying in Paris and, on his return to Jerusalem in 1951, held a one-man show in the Artist's House. A volume of sketches dealing with life in the pre-military units for Israel's high-school students, *Beohalei Gadna,* on the lines of his earlier collection of wartime sketches, was published later that year.

In 1952, Mikra Studios of Tel Aviv published an album, *Jerusalem,* consisting of water colors and pen-and-ink sketches by Yossi Stern. At this time, he became a regular contributor to a number of daily and weekly newspapers. Since 1954, he has made regular tours of the art centers of Europe in France, Holland, Italy and Greece. He had one-man shows at the Rinah Galley, Jerusalem (1950), at the Chamerinski Galley, Tel Aviv (1963) and at Bet Haam, Jerusalem (1964). A collection of his work entitled *Yossi Stern,* was published by the Israeli

Publishing Institute in 1964. In 1966, he spent a year in the United States, exhibiting his work and studying.

It has often been said that there is no Israeli "school" of art. There are many Israeli artists, but no specific style or approach which can be identified as uniquely Israeli. This may be because of the great diversity of the population, and the intermingling of many national cultures and philosophies. Yossi Stern, in his deep love for his people, and his desire to communicate to—and for—them, uses the diversity of expression which is, after all, an echo of the diversity which is Israel.

Stern's wanderings, sketchpad in hand, in the streets of Jerusalem result in paintings like this

HERMANN STRUCK
1876-1944

In thousands of Jewish homes all over the world hangs a bronze etching of Theodor Herzl made by the artist Hermann Struck. The inner harmony and noble character of the great Jewish leader are the prominent features of the etching, made in May 1903, about 15 months before Herzl's death. No other work of art has so completely captured the essence of Herzl — his devotion and concern for his people, his aspirations for their national redemption, his quiet, patient nobility. It is no wonder that so many Jews have found comfort and inspiration in Struck's reproduction of his face.

Hermann Struck used to say that Herzl made an unforgettable impression on him with his graceful beauty, his majestic bearing, his sincere charm and his flashing visionary eyes, all immortalized in Struck's work. Many other famous people responded to Struck's insight and talent and asked him to do their portraits. Rabbis, authors, poets, scholars, statesmen and businessmen sought his services, and such great men as Ibsen, Einstein and Freud gladly sat for him as models for stone-cuts, bronze etchings and lithographs. In all of them Struck displayed that same craftsmanship and artistry, that capacity to capture the inner essence of personality displayed in the famous Herzl etching.

Haim Aharon (or Hermann) Struck was born in 1876 and grew up in Berlin. His first exhibition, held when he was 23, won him an important prize as well as membership in England's Royal Art Society. He traveled widely, gathering impressions wherever he went. In 1903 he paid a visit to Palestine and eventually settled there in 1923.

With the outbreak of World War I in 1914, the German High Command appointed Struck expert on Jewish affairs in Eastern Europe. There followed the most formative experience of his life — meeting the Jews of Eastern Europe. He who had wandered

"Theodor Herzl" by Struck

over Europe in search of artistic experience suddenly came face-to-face with his own people. From Vilna he traveled throughout the ghettos of the Diaspora, dealing with the problems of Jewish refugees. When the war finally ended he joined the German delegation at the Versailles peace talks to press the claims of the refugees. He used his time in Paris for artistic purposes too and after the conclusion of the Peace Conference wrote an important book on impressionist art.

Due to his exceptional talents, Struck always held a place of distinction in the art world. Other Jewish artists, notably Joseph Israels in Holland and Liebermann in Germany, also worked on Jewish themes, but Struck is always considered the most truly "Jewish" artist of the three. In the ferment of cosmopolitan artistic life that was Berlin, where many chose to assimilate, Struck remained true to the Jewish religion. He was scrupulous in the observance of the commandments, set aside regular hours for learning Torah and strived for spiritual purity. The aim of his life was first to live as a Jew, and then to immortalize on canvas the faces of a few outstanding individuals whose essence was such that they served to represent the entire Jewish nation. All the characteristics which epitomized the Jew during his time — humility and profundity, grace and charm, love of the Torah and the joy of fulfilling the commandments — all these found their true interpreter in Struck. Struck lived all his life in a Jewish environment and remained true to the spiritual beliefs and practices that had animated his people for thousands of years. Loyalty to Judaism was the chief theme of both his life and art.

It was for this reason that he turned for inspiration to Eastern Europe, in spite of his Western education and upbringing. The unexpected meeting with Eastern Jewry during the war brought him into direct contact with a Judaism that was alive and fresh,

Hermann Struck at work. The inscription reads: "To Mr. Martin Birnbaum with best regards. Hermann. Berlin, 9.9.1912"

Frau Marie ... mit besten Grüßen Hermann ...

Berlin 9.9. 1912

simple but noble. It was a healthy, proud Judaism and it transformed the artist's conception of his role. Thereafter, he drew the spiritual awareness and good sense of these Eastern Jews, their orthodoxy, their sufferings and their good-heartedness. They supplied a rich field for his talent and he tilled it diligently.

ARTHUR SZYK
1895-1951

Arthur Szyk, the son of a minor textile manufacturer in Lodz, Poland, was a hard-working talented man who found his knowledge of medieval art illumination useful in the modern struggle for existence of the Jewish people.

Even as a boy, making letters with tiny drawings as part of them was Arthur's idea of fun. No doubt many Jewish craftsmen still follow the ancient trade of copying the Torah word for word, letter for letter, but Arthur Szyk raised this kind of craftsmanship to an artistic level seldom achieved.

The Haggadah, one of his most famous works, took him years. The first letters of paragraphs were in gold ink, the rest in various colors. All of the original 240 copies of the work were immediately sold at more than $500 each and the original was presented to the King of England.

Szyk wrote and drew books, scrolls, documents, histories. His illumination of the famous Law of Kalish, which granted Jews rights in Poland, was both artistic and popular. It gives us a graphic history of Polish Jewry through its magnificent array of pictures. His careful writing and illustrating of the *Book of Esther, Song of Songs, The Book of Job, the Rubaiyat,* and *Andersen's Tales* added to his reputation throughout the world. One of his best-known achievements is a Scroll of Israel's Declaration of Independence, both in Hebrew and English, which hangs framed in many homes today.

Szyk was a Polish patriot as well as a loyal Jew, and served as an officer in the Polish Army. He believed the Jews and Poles could learn to understand each other, in spite of the Poles' traditional anti-Semitism. He was commissioned by the Polish government to draw a miniature picture of the American Revolutionary War as a gift for President Franklin D. Roosevelt.

Szyk's name was taken from the initials of the name of Rabbi Shimon Kaznelbogen, whom his father loved and admired. Arthur knew Hebrew and Yiddish as well as Polish, and spent some time in Palestine before World War I. He studied art in Paris and Poland, where he settled. After the fall of Poland in 1939, he came to Amer-

"Hillel" by Szyk

Arthur Szyk, left, painting the famous poster stamp design shown below. The British Armed Forces are represented by a modern St. George slaying the evil dragon of Nazism which has Freedom in chains

ALL HOPE ABANDON
YE WHO ENTER HERE...

"Getto"

וַאֶעֱבֹר עָלַיִךְ וָאֶרְאֵ
מִתְבּוֹסֶסֶת בְּדָמָיִךְ
וָאֹמַר לָךְ: בְּדָמַיִךְ חֲיִי
וָאֹמַר לָךְ: בְּדָמַיִךְ חֲיִי
יחזקאל 17

N.Y. ARTHUR SZYK

ica. Szyk had been known and liked everywhere for his illustrations. With the attack on his people by the Nazis, he became a political artist. His caricatures of Hitler, Goebbels and Goering, are unforgettable. He wrote a book, *The New Order,* did caricatures for newspapers, magazines, pamphlets, posters, and did everything to help save his people, to arouse the world to an awareness of the Nazi crimes. Whether his work could be strictly classified as art no longer interested him.

"Adam Czerniakow" by Arthur Szyk (Left)

The leaders of the World War II Axis—Italy's Mussolini, Germany's Hitler, and Hirohito of Japan—are depicted by Szyk as ruthless gangsters

"I'm not an artist," he said, "I'm a soldier. My art is a means. My aim: struggle, war, not only against Hitler alone, but against the Germany that has allowed this Hitler to rise. I want holy revenge."

Szyk's political drawings and caricatures were sometimes sharply satirical, sometimes sentimental, sometimes bitter. They moved people, as they were meant to do. Szyk's wide-eyed starving child with a star of David sewn on his baggy rags, staring through barbed wire, is unforgettable.

Szyk used his paintbrush as a soldier uses a gun. He attacked Russia while it was still friendly with Germany, as well as the Vichy French pro-German government, and his attacks stung, with the result that he was often attacked himself. But he had some important friends too, including President Roosevelt, who hung some of his caricatures in his Hyde Park home.

According to Szyk, his ability to caricature was a Jewish gift. In a caricature, the artist must not only draw the likeness of a person with only a few strokes of the pen, but present his personality as well. "Because I'm a Jew, heart and soul, I am an analyzer, body and soul — I enter the hearts of things."

LESSER URY
1863-1931

Lesser Ury was a tragic, bitter, lonely figure. When he died at the age of 69, he was unaware of the festivities which Germany was planning in his honor, in the form of an exhibition at Berlin's National Gallery.

When Ury came to Berlin in 1885 he brought with him the new French theory of painting — Impressionism. His first exhibit was greeted with ridicule, as public and critics alike were unprepared to accept this totally new approach to painting. Both in his life and his art Lesser Ury was a solitary man who stubbornly continued along his independent road, always trying to find a new means of expression for his unique vision of the old familiar subjects.

As far back as 1881, when he was in Brussels, Ury was filling his canvasses with Jewish subjects, such as *The Destruction of Jerusalem.* Unlike other painters of the time he did not exploit theatrical pathos. Rather he imbued his pictures with a feeling of the quiet nobility of the nameless people he drew, who radiated light and strength despite their cruel fate. His works tried to show how a specific historical portrayal contained within it that which was also universal and eternal. He wanted to express the fate of his nation and his people in his work.

In his painting *Jeremiah,* he depicts an old man lying under the night sky, a sky so wide and unending that it strikes the viewer with a feeling of awe. The old man lies on a block of stone and is lit by a crown of stars from above. His eyes carry an accusing question to the infinite heights. The prophet seems to be saying to his Master, "Crumble me, Lord, and I am nothing. Strengthen me and I can carry on."

Moses was another subject that Ury painted — Moses, standing opposite the sinning, obstinate masses, opposite the generation that had grown up in slavery yet had been honored with the words of the Lord from Mount Sinai.

In *Jacob Blessing Benjamin* we see a youth on his knees before an old man who bends over him, as if protecting him, his gnarled hands covering the child's head. We see here not only the concern

"Winter Scene" by Lesser Ury

of a father for the fate of his child, but a highly religious picture as well.

As one of the first Impressionists in Germany, Lesser received no recognition, although three other painters — Liebermann, Corinth and Sefulget — were eventually accepted and became some of the most important representatives of German painting at that time. Even though the fate of the Jewish nation occupied Lesser's mind and canvasses almost all of his life, he did not receive praise or recognition from the Jews for his devotion to a subject which should have been dear to them.

In addition to Jewish subjects, Lesser was one of the great interpreters of the life of the city. His works eternalized the turbulence and beauty of modern cities, and although they were not accepted for many years, towards the end of his life Lesser was proclaimed "the Glorifier of the Capital of the Third Reich."

He was a poet of moods, using the entire spectrum of colors to reflect the richness and suffering of the soul. His life was a long chain of disappointments and pain, but his great insight and pioneering spirit earned him a place as one of the most important artists of our time.

WILLIAM ZORACH
1887-1966

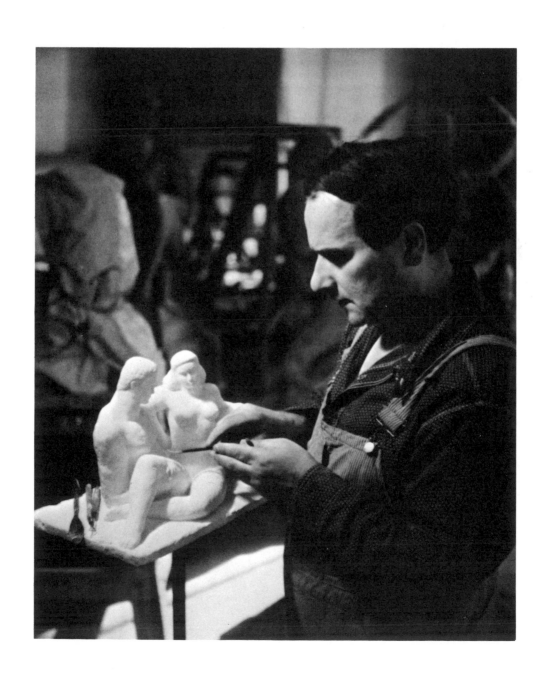

"A true artist can make raw materials come to life with the touch of his hand. Others are not artists but merely artisans who can complete works, which, however, do not come to life. The amateur has a tendency to confuse the two and forget that without artistic content there is no justification for the work," William Zorach wrote in his book, *True Sculpture,* in which he set down his view of the world of art. He worked in stone, marble, granite, wood and bronze, understood the limitations of each material and knew how to match material with subject. His aim was not to create a living being in the naturalistic or realistic sense, but to imbue the material with a feeling of individual life and experience. His works were in many ways similar to those of the ancient artists of Egypt, Greece and China, although he did not try to imitate them. All his work is based on an individual interpretation of eternal principles of sculpting. He longed always to do the monumental.

A school instructor recognized Zorach's extraordinary talent for impressionist drawing and painting and he recommended him to a lithographer, who could train him further in another medium. Zorach was enchanted by this new world of expression. But he longed to go to Paris, which in 1910 was in full artistic revolution. He worked there for several years, identifying himself with the new currents. He was successful enough with his brush and his pencils, but when he later returned to America he was nagged by the feeling that he was in the wrong medium, and that he was not achieving complete fulfillment. As always, Zorach loved to experiment, and in 1917 he tried his hand at wood carving for the first time. He was excited by this new material and the challenge it offered. He dropped his painting and in 1922, at the relatively late age of thirty-five, began to build a new artistic career. This daring decision — he had never had any formal instruction in sculpting — was a factor in his success, as he was able to evolve his own individual style without being hampered by traditional dogma. By 1930 Zorach had become known in some circles as the most important contemporary American sculptor in the United States.

"Myra" by Zorach

Zorach often began working in stone with no specific image in mind of what the end product would be, allowing his artistic intent to blend with the material's potential and natural characteristics. He also used another important artistic expression — spontaneity, letting himself be guided by the material he was working on as well as his own inspiration. Zorach always sought to bring out the universal form through individual expression. The general, undefined, and blurred shape hinting at its subject is more fitting for sculpture than compact, balanced and precise delineation. He was able to give his work a three-dimensional quality, which forced the viewer to keep moving around the sculpture in order to capture its complete meaning.

In 1923, Zorach was commissioned to do a monumental work, and he created the figure of the *Spirit of the Dance,* which stands now in front of the largest movie theater in the world, Radio City Music Hall. He prepared the model first in plaster, and then in aluminum, which at that time was a new medium. He mastered the technique of working with metals and succeeded in creating the illusion of living, flowing movement within the static material of the metal.

Zorach was a consummate master of the basic demands of his art — he was a technician able to interpret the deepest human qualities through a complete understanding of his materials.

One of his favorite subjects was cats, and his statue of cats, in hewn Swedish stone, was bought by the Metropolitan Museum of New York, which had to outbid eighty other museums throughout the world for this work. Zorach also excelled in sculpting well-known historical figures such as Benjamin Franklin, a marvellous marble statue, seven-and-a-half feet high, which stands in the halls of the central Post Office in Washington. For this work he made a study of everything related to the character of Franklin, his temperament, his dress, his tastes, so that his interpretation would reflect all the basic traits and qualities of the man.

Zorach was an active and inspiring teacher at the New York

"Christ" by Zorach

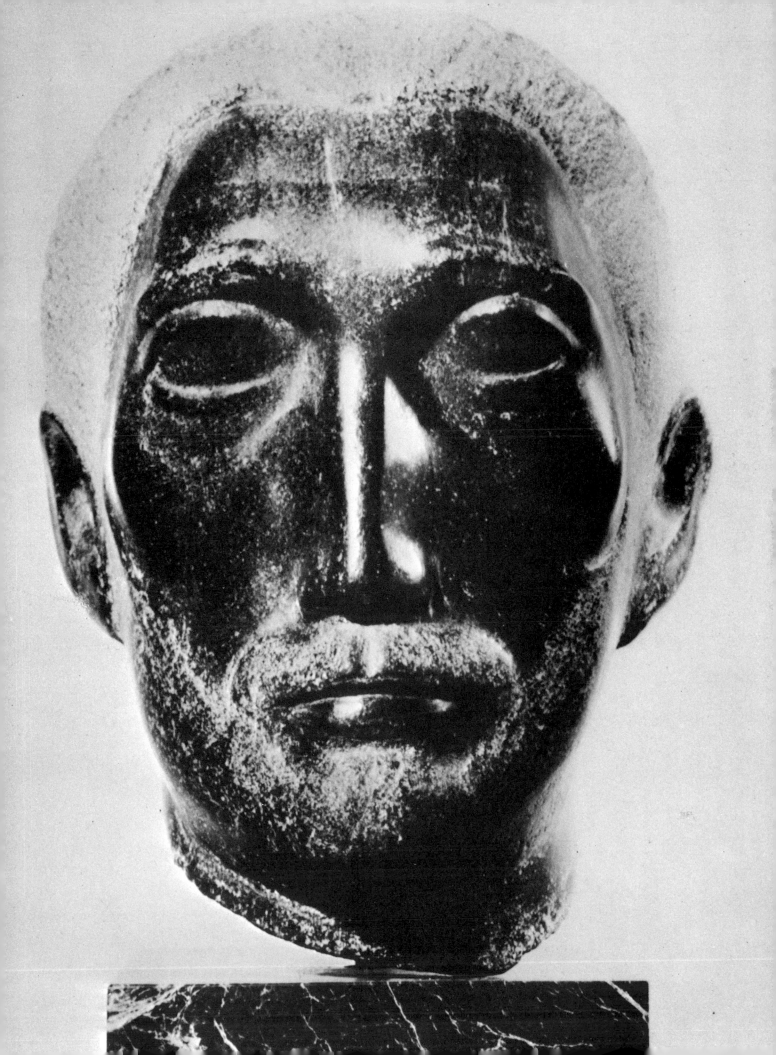

Art Students League, and wrote several important books on his artistic approach and vision. He stands, with Jacques Lipchitz, as one of the finest plastic artists in America.

INDEX